Transforming the Mature Information Technology Organization:

Reenergizing and Motivating People

Transforming the Mature Information Technology Organization:
Reenergizing and Motivating People

Robert A. Zawacki
University of Colorado and
KPMG Peat Marwick

Carol A. Norman
Telephone Express

Paul A. Zawacki
Zawacki and Associates

Paul D. Applegate
KPMG Peat Marwick

EAGLESTAR
Publishing
Colorado Springs, CO 80919
1995

Transforming the mature
information technology

STAR Organization™ is a registered trademark of Zawacki and
    Associates

Graphics illustrations: Marc Jenesel
Cover design: Don Seegmiller
Printer: Sprint Press, Inc.

Library of Congress Catalog Card Number: 95-61043

ISBN 0-9646910-0-0

Printed in the United States of America
10 9 8 7 6 5 4 3 2 1

Preface

Our experience is that many of the current change programs are good, proper, and necessary. However, the largest percentage of these change programs are failing because IT leaders and consultants underestimate the resistance by the human element to implement effective change. Our organization of the future (STAR) places strong emphasis on customer service and time-based competition. Further, you cannot have external customer service until you have internal customer service. Internal customer service succeeds when people feel valued. People feel valued when the majority of the variables of the STAR organization are in place and reinforced by its leadership. Then, people add value to the bottom-line. This book contains our experiences in coaching IT organizations through this journey and contains numerous guidelines and checklists to help IT leadership transform their organizations.

The original idea for this book was an outcome of a meeting about two years ago, when we were discussing the need in information technology to design learning organizations that maximize the fit between the individual and the organization and between the organization and its environment. Also, we talked about our observations that many articles, books, and consultants were making prescriptive statements about how to design the learning organization that leveraged the use of technology while motivating people to increased productivity.

As we reviewed the proliferation of *prescriptive* and *how to* business books during the last few years, we concluded that writers were doing a fairly good job of describing the changing business environment, but when confronted with how to design a learning organization and mobilize employees (reenergizing people) after downsizing, they were not meeting the needs of their clients - the line managers. One of our clients in a major East Coast manufacturing company expressed this typical frustration when he said, "I just read one of the latest and best selling books on the learning organization, but please help me find a book that tells me how to do it." Further, both individual contributors and management were expressing a deep cynicism towards any new change program which usually had a flavor of *the latest quick fix* or *micro wave management*!

At about the same time, we were experimenting with the learning organization (STAR) in information technology-driven companies, and having some major successes in designing and implementing the organization of the future. Additionally, international publications such as **Personnel Journal, Datamation, Information Week**, and **Computerworld** began to interview us for their stories and also were asking us to write articles in their journals about our consulting experiences. Further, numerous conference organizers such as the **Amdahl User Group, International Functional Point User Group, Help Desk Institute, SIM**, and the **Conference Board** asked us to share our experiences with many chief information officers and senior IT leaders. Those keynotes were always received with great enthusiasm and encouragement to share our experiences with a wider audience. All of these forces came together to motivate us to write this book.

About the Authors

Dr. Robert A. Zawacki (Ph.D. University of Washington) is Professor Emeritus of Management and International Business at the University of Colorado and KPMG Peat Marwick Distinguished Scholar in Residence. Also, he is the president of Zawacki and Associates, a research firm specializing in information technology organizations. He is the former Dean of the College of Business & Administration, University of Colorado, Colorado Springs and prior to that he was on the faculty of the Air Force Academy. He is the author of 15 books and more than 200 articles/keynotes in information systems. His book **Motivating and Managing Computer Personnel** is considered the definitive statement on the people side of IT. Also, his book **Organization Development and Transformation: Implementing Effective Change** has been used by over 400 universities world wide.

He is the keynote speaker at numerous international IT meetings and consulted with over 100 international organizations. He is married to the former Jimmie Louise Beaird and they have 6 grown children and 5 grandchildren. They make their home at the base of Pikes Peak in Colorado Springs.

Carol A. Norman is the Major Account Manager at Telephone Express in Colorado Springs, Colorado. At Telephone Express the major accounts team delivers premium level service to the top level customers in telecommunication and information age services such as the Internet. Previously, she worked at Digital Equipment Corporation, where she was as major account representative for NASA, Citibank, U.S. Postal Service and Reuters. She is a Certified Novell Engineer and worked extensively designing, implementing, and troubleshooting LANs and WANs.

She managed or worked in self directed teams for the past 12 years. She was involved with growing a self directed team from 1 to 40 people. Her research activities focus on self directed teams and she wrote 11 articles in that area. She currently teaches graduate and undergraduate courses in organizational management at the University of Colorado, Colorado Springs. She received her undergraduate degree in Management Information Systems with a minor in Computer Science and has a MBA in Organizational Management. Both degrees are from the University of Colorado.

Paul A. Zawacki has worked with and consulted in the various disciplines of information technology since 1981. For the last 10 years, he concentrated his efforts on leading edge network management technologies and project leadership. He has been actively researching management issues in information technology for over 15 years and has authored two articles on these topics. He received a B.S. in business administration from the University of Colorado where his emphasis was Information Systems Management.

Paul D. Applegate is a partner in the Strategic Services consulting practice of KPMG Peat Marwick LLP based in Denver, Colorado. He has 21 years of experience in the areas of information system planning, system design and integration, and operations performance improvement in a wide variety of industries.

Prior to joining KPMG, he was MIS Director of a manufacturing and distribution company. In that capacity, he was responsible for identification of business process improvement opportunities, implementation of redesigned business processes, and evaluation, selection, and implementation of new enterprise-wide systems. He was also Executive Vice President of a software firm which specialized in financial and distribution systems.

Acknowledgments

We wish to acknowledge our deep debt to the following people who contributed to proofreading the book, cover design, project management, and making many helpful suggestions: Jimmie L. Zawacki, Helen Beaird, Mary Ann Zawacki, Karen Hawkins, Don Seegmiller, Jennifer Seegmiller, Nicole Seegmiller, Mark A. Zawacki and Martha L. Seegmiller.

Contents

PART I

TRANSFORMING TO THE COMPETITIVE ORGANIZATION

Chapter 1

Transforming from the Mature (Old) to the New Organization

Introduction

After decades of working, consulting, researching, and writing about information technology (IT) organizations we believe the two paramount issues that information technology leaders are struggling with are: (1) **what will the IT organization of the future look like,** and (2) **how to implement effective change.** In this chapter we will discuss the mature (bureaucratic) organization and the organization of the future (STAR). In the remaining chapters we will discuss the issue of implementing effective change by recognizing the relationship between technology, structure, environment, and people to design a high performance organization that produces outstanding business results.

Actually, these two issues facing IT leaders in the 1990s, are inter-related because many IT leaders are attempting to add value to their organizations. As they attempt to add value, they are having difficulty implementing very innovative and participative change programs in mature organizations designed for the 1950s - not the learning organizations designed for the 1990s. Thus, as IT leaders attempt to implement change programs in the traditional organizational forms designed for the 1950s, they don't stop and reflect enough on the challenges of change programs, what is necessary to support that change program as they venture forward, and the forces shaping the organization for the future.

Forces Shaping the IT Organization of the Future. Listed below are some of the macro and micro forces shaping the organization of the future:

1. Global markets and manufacturing facilities are requiring that business units have immediate access to data. Many businesses are very close to or are actually technology companies. The computer architecture of client-server permits business

units to change faster than the older mainframes and legacy systems.

2. A slow realization by IT leadership that the largest percentage of future increases in productivity will ultimately depend upon the trust between IT leadership and individual contributors.

3. The computer became the nervous system of the organization, permitting entire layers of management to be replaced with local and wide area networks. In the past, middle management was primarily responsible for processing information used in the decision making process by top management. Now that information, because of the PC and networks, is immediately available to all people without the need for middle managers to process the information. In the future, the organization will become even flatter with extremely wide spans of control.

4. Technology is moving far faster than the ability of IT leadership to shift organizational vision, values, strategic goals, tactical goals, and behaviors. As a consequence, IT leaders must pay critical attention to transforming the organization while maintaining customer focus. CIOs maybe losing the battle. A recent study by the Standish Group International indicates that only 16.2 percent of all software projects are completed on time and on budget, and the figure drops to 9 percent for large companies. Thus, software development projects are in chaos.[1]

5. As IT leaders work at maintaining a customer focus and adding value to the bottom line of the business units, they are reducing staff, while attempting to maintain, or even increase, productivity. Thus, many IT leaders turn to the next *quick fix* or latest management tenets (fads) as the answer.

6. We believe the answer is **not** in the latest *quick fix* or *micro wave management*, rather, the IT organization that will survive in the 1990s by adding value to the bottom line of the business units, IT leaders must design an organization that is fluid, adaptable, always learning, and responsive to the changing business environment. Many business leaders and con-

sultants believe that the primary contribution of IT leaders of the future will be to design the organization that will best support the business vision and strategies.

Expertise in organization design will be a critical skill - a skill that will require considerable technical knowledge about how to analyze, modify, and stimulate the behavior of complex human systems.[2]

The Old Mature Organization and the Future Organization (STAR)

The mature organization (the present organization for many firms) is based upon a bureaucratic model that has a value system and a specific structural design such as division of labor, span of control, job descriptions, business functions, and organizational charts (and pictures) on the office walls. The organization of the future has many names but more characteristics in common than differences. Some of the names that are presently *tossed around in print* are the horizontal organization, the learning organization, the network organization, the unglued organization, the core competencies organization, organizational architecture, the time based competition organization, the virtual organization, the shamrock organization, the high velocity environment[3] and ours which we call the STAR organization.

STAR is an acronym for **S**trategic goals, in a constant state of **T**ransition, **A**nd in constant **R**enewal and learning. Thus, the STAR organization is a vary fluid organization that is closely connected to the environment and customers, a very flat organization that is designed around learning teams, and is organized around process - not function or task. In the IT organization of the future, the focus will be on the project culture.[4]

From Incremental to Random Change

Before we discuss the future IT organization, we believe it is critical to have a discussion on the paradigm shift that is taking place in the change literature. Previously we mentioned that IT leaders are attempting to implement change in the 1990s in traditional IT organizations designed for the 1950s. What did we mean by that statement?

One of the main reasons for still working in mature organizations designed for the 1950s is that IT people may make the wrong assumptions about change. In the past, change flowed along a reasonably predictable course and individual contributors in the

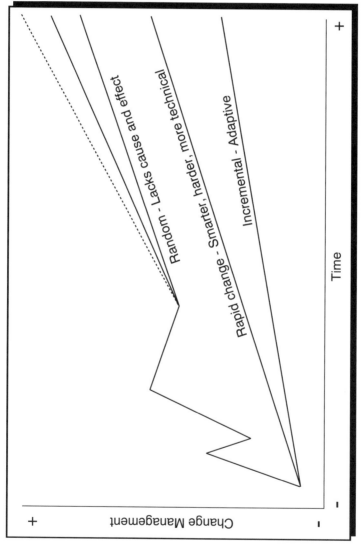

Figure 1-1. Historical Response to Change.

IT organization adjusted by working harder and smarter to stay ahead of the changes. Recently, however, organizations are facing high-speed change that is frequently changing the direction, focus, and behaviors of individual contributors.[5]

Information technology professionals have experienced three different change/impact paradigms from the 1950s to the present.[6] First, when more effective and ever-larger mainframes were introduced in the 1950s and 1960s, data processing people were in control, basically telling the business units what they needed and when the business units would get it! We call this period of *incremental change* the tell-and-sell period. Although there was change during this period, and people were threatened by the change, the key is to understand that people had **time** to adjust.

During the 1970s and 1980s change became more *rapid* and information systems people stayed ahead of the changes by working harder (hours worked per week in the U.S. is still increasing), smarter (computer assisted manufacturing, object oriented programming, etc.), and introducing more technology, such as midrange computers, microcomputers, local area networks, and wide area networks. During this period of rapid change, customers became more computer literate, used more user-friendly software, and the customer began to question the effectiveness of I/S. Shared influence (partnerships) between business units and I/S increased in planning for the purchasing of technology and establishing priorities. Further, there was some general movement toward downsizing staff and empowering employees. During this period of rapid change, the business unit's views toward I/S was changing and the **time** to adjust to change was decreasing.

Line 3 in Figure 1-1 illustrates what is happening in the 1990s which is a true paradigm shift. Change is becoming more *random* and appears to the individual contributor to lack cause and effect. We call this decade of high velocity change *continuous discontinuous change*.

Three brief examples highlight our contention about continuous discontinuous change lacking cause and effect. First, we became aware of a family whose son attended a state university at some family financial sacrifice. The son majored in aeronautical engineering, studied hard, and graduated first in his engineering class. As an honor graduate, he only had two job interviews and received one job offer to track government contracts on a computer. When he entered the university, aeronautical engineers were in demand; when he graduated after the ending of the cold war, there was little demand for aeronautical engineers. To him and his family this change lacked cause and effect. The old rewards for hard work, motivation, and commitment no longer applied in this period of random change!

A second example - an engineer joined a large computer manufacturing company after graduating from a top engineering school in software engineering. When he joined the firm, he was told that he was on the "fast track" and had an excellent opportunity for rapid advancement in the firm. For the next eight years he worked long hours, received outstanding performance reports, and was promoted to first-line management ahead of his peers. When another company purchased his company and consolidated information systems departments, he was told that the new organization no longer needed his services. To him, with a wife, two children, and a new home, this decision lacked cause and effect. Further, the new company gave him no time to adjust to the change.

A third example is IBM. This firm was very successful building and delivering large computer systems to clients during the periods represented by lines 1 and 2 above. However, when a new paradigm of change (random), the computer giant was not flexible enough to perform effectively on line 3. Further, they did not have the individual and organizational learning processes in place to reflect on their decisions and change their behaviors. In fact, the very behaviors that made IBM successful on line 1 and 2, became a liability on line 3 because the old behaviors (which had cause and effect) kept people from seeing the new paradigm and designing an organization that will be successful on line 3.

Behavior and Change

Chris Argyris, in a 1991 Harvard Business Review article,[7] elaborates on this idea that the behaviors which are successful on line 1 and 2 now become a liability on line 3. Further, he states that the smarter people are and the more rapid their advancement in the organization, the harder it is for them to learn. Argyris calls the old process on lines 1 and 2 "single-loop learning" and the new process "double-loop learning" and suggests that the primary need in the organization of the future is teaching smart people how to learn. Some authors extend the idea of individual learning and see:

> **. . .organization learning as the principal process by which management innovation occurs. In fact, I would argue that the rate at which individuals and organizations learn may become the only sustainable competitive advantage, especially in knowledge-intensive industries.**[2]

Thus, IT professionals must unlearn their old behavior before they can learn new behavior. An example is the recent rise in the use of teams in IT. Now we believe that teams will be one of the building blocks of the future organization; however, after eight years of research on teams in IT we discovered that only one-third of self-directed teams add any value to the bottom line.[5] Our research documented that many organizations were implementing teams and the reward system was still based upon single-loop learning which doomed the teams to failure. For self-directed teams to be successful, IT leaders need a good plan, are willing to stay the course, change the evaluation system to a 360 degree performance appraisal system (see Chapter 5), and have some percentage of the merit increase based upon peer input. Behaviors that are rewarded are repeated![8]

Old (Mature) and New Values

Successful leaders and organizations have values that promote a feeling by the organizational participants of consistency and stability in a period of random change. As we move from incremental and rapid change to random change we must *dump the old bureaucratic paternalistic organization for the future organization (STAR)*. Thus, an understanding of the old values, the manifestations of those values, and the new (STAR) values are crucial as a foundation for reenergizing the mature IT organization.[9]

MATURE AND NEW VALUES [9]	
Mature Values	**Manifestations or Outcomes**
1. Little personal investment in IT vision, values, and objectives.	They are the leader's values - not mine.
2. People need a leader to direct them.	Hierarchy of authority and control.
3. Keep the boss happy.	Real issues don't surface at meetings.
4. If something goes wrong, blame someone else.	Appeal procedures become over-formalized.
5. Don't make waves.	Innovation is not widespread but in the hands of a few technologists.
6. Tomorrow will be just like today.	People swallow their frustrations: "I can't do anything - it's leaderships' responsibility to save the ship."
7. People don't like change/they like security.	Job descriptions, division of labor, and little empires.
8. People will avoid work if possible.	Close supervision, job descriptions, and centralization.
9. Poor performance is glossed over or handled arbitrarily.	Do my job and look the other way when I see errors.
10. Learning is difficult or ignored. They dismiss the ideas of peers.	Single loop-learning.
11. Status and boxes on the organizational chart are more important than solving problems.	People are polite, non-conformity is frowned upon and the boss is always correct.
12. People feel de-valued.	People do the bare minimum to get by - they keep their head down.
13. People compete when they need to cooperate.	Conflicts develop and are not discussed or surfaced.
14. People feel the need for security and are locked into boring and meaningless work.	People come to staff meetings and do not contribute - they say why bother.
15. People can't be trusted to do the right thing.	IT leaders feel alone in trying to establish a vision and objectives. Their orders do not always get implemented.

Figure 1-2. Mature and New Values.

MATURE AND NEW VALUES [9]	
STAR Values	Manifestations and Outcomes
1. Vision, values and objectives are shared and owned by all IT individual contributors and business units.	These are my values.
2. People are capable of managing themselves within the vision, values and objectives.	Hierarchy is replaced with self directed teams.
3. Keep the customer happy.	Customer driven performance.
4. The buck stops here.	People address real problems and find synergistic solutions.
5. Make waves.	Waves result in innovation.
6. Nobody knows what tomorrow will bring.	Constant learning to prepare for the unknown future.
7. Although random change upsets our behavior patterns, we learn and adjust.	Change is an opportunity to grow.
8. People want meaningful work.	Learning new technology, given autonomy and feedback, we grow.
9. Poor performance is addressed by the teams.	We learn from our mistakes and move forward.
10. Learning is rewarded.	Peer and customer feedback is sought out. Double-loop learning.
11. People go to who has the answer.	People work to achieve a correct solution and are not worried about what management will think.
12. People feel valued.	They add value to the product and customer.
13. People know when to compete and cooperate.	They collaborate with the customer and each other.
14. People believe their competencies are their security.	They seek out new technology and contribute.
15. People can be trusted to do the right thing.	People concentrate on quality products delivered on time in a cost effective manner while having fun!

Figure 1-2 continued. Mature and New Values.

Leverage Points for IT Leaders

Previously we discussed the mature (old) organization as a bureaucratic and control centered structure that was designed for the business environment of the 1950s and we also discussed the manifestations and outcomes of this model. Unfortunately, many

IT leaders are still using this structure to deliver the business solutions demanded by their customers. Further, as IT leaders attempt to implement change programs such as total quality management, self directed teams, and business process reengineering, which are excellent change programs; however, to be totally successful

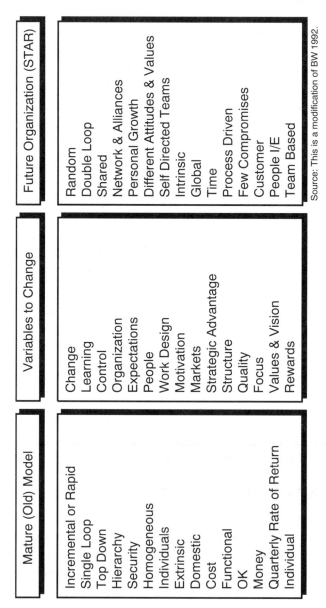

Figure 1-3. Model of the Future Organization.

Source: This is a modification of BW 1992.

these programs should be implemented in an organization designed for the 1990s.

Next we briefly introduced the future organization that is labeled as the STAR, horizontal, and learning organization. The future organization is designed to maximize effectiveness in periods of random change. Basically, it is a very flat, team based, adaptable and self correcting structure that is in a constant state of transformation.

In the old organization, leaders developed a vision of an end state and then implemented a managed change program to reach that end state. In the future organization, because of the increase in destabilizing events in the business environment, IT leaders are on a journey without an end state. Thus, to have a sustained competitive advantage, IT leaders must design an organization that is constantly learning and adjusting to *continuous discontinuous* change which we label as random change. Figure 1-3 depicts the mature (old) organization, the variables the IT leader can change to leverage the change program, and the future organization (STAR).

Variables to Change. Based on our experience, IT leaders are searching for models that will help them achieve focus and alignment in their organizations in this decade of *continuous discontinuous* change. Figure 2-2 actually lists the variables that IT leaders should be aware of and can change to load the change program for success. We recommend that IT leaders select two or three variables as the drivers for their change effort and continuously emphasize those leverage points to demonstrate the importance of the change effort and that the change effort has top level support. For example, an East Coast financial institution decided to use self directed teams to move from the mature organization to the STAR organization. Their change effort focused on the communication and training of the individual contributors on how to design and implement teams, communicated with the customer how the teams would be customer driven and increase contact with the customer, and put in place a team based performance appraisal and reward system to reinforce the change program. Because time and financial resources are scarce in today's IT organization, IT leaders should use the 80/20 rule and concentrate on the leverage variables that will accelerate the change program.

From the Old to the STAR Values. We already discussed the old and STAR values; however, IT leaders must recognize that their vision and value system are the foundation for building the learning organization. Many IT leaders take their leadership team off-site and work on vision and values, they even may communicate the vision and values to their individual contributors and post these on the office walls. However, once the values are communicated and posted, many IT organizations are seduced by the daily crises at the expense of living their values. Using today's slang: *IT leaders must not only talk the talk but must be able to walk the walk!* Software engineers are very sensitive to their leaders' behaviors and are looking for leadership behaviors that are consistent with the STAR values.

From Incremental to Rapid Change. As organizations move from incremental, through rapid change, and into random change, people have a tremendous need to *hang on to the past* because they have been successful in the mature organization (conditioning) and they know what the rewards are. As organizations move into random change, individual contributors can experience confusion, denial, shock or even a re-orientation. Thus, people have a basic need for stability while successful leaders are introducing change as a proactive response to the rapidly changing environment. The needs of healthy individual contributors (stability) is in basic conflict with the needs of healthy organizations (instability) to adjust quickly to a changing environment. Figure 1-4 is a model of individual responses, both reactive and proactive, to the three types of change. IT leaders must recognize that all people resist change, why people resist change, and how to help them adjust to the change process.

From Single-Loop to Double-Loop Learning. Single-loop learning is when individual contributors perform effectively in the mature organization, are rewarded for their performance, they and the organization interpret the reward as success and they repeat the behavior. The smarter people are, the faster they respond to this process and the harder it is for IT leaders to change this process. For example, assume an IT organization is implementing project teams and obviously want the teams to work effectively to maintain or even increase the quality of their product. There is a

Individual Response to Change	Types of Change		
	Incremental	Rapid	Random
Proactive	Small and planned changes, i.e., a new training program or a one-shot off site meeting	Larger planned changes, i.e., TQM, teams, or a new performance appraisal system	Renewal, re-orientation, and reenergizing
Reactive	Contentment and some adaptation	Confusion and some benchmarking (work long hours, harder, and more technology)	Denial, shock and suprise

Source: This is a modification of David A. Nadler, Robert B. Shaw, and A. Elise Walton, **Discontinuous Change** (San Francisco.: Jossey-Bass Publishers, 1994), page 24.

Figure 1-4. Individual Response to Change.

high probability that the high performers will continue to excel individually while giving lip service to the team concept because they realize that they are still evaluated and rewarded individually. Double-loop learning consists of an unfreezing process before a new change program is implemented. To introduce double-loop learning in the IT organization of the future, IT leaders must introduce a team based performance appraisal and reward system. When smart people see that the reward system has changed, they learn quickly - they are quick takes!

Shared Control. It is very difficult for some IT leaders to share control with other leaders and individual contributors because during periods of incremental and rapid change they have been effective in delivering information technology. However, when people and organizations are required to adjust to random change, many IT leaders believe that they can make the correct decision quicker than a team. The missing link in this line of reasoning is that IT leaders also need to develop commitment to the decision. Increased commitment, higher quality decisions, and understanding come from individual participation in the decision-making process.

Organization Structure. Many mature IT organizations have 5 or 6 levels of hierarchy. In the organization of the future there will be 3 layers and at the most 4 layers. The typical chain-of-command will be programmer, project leader, and director. Also, spans of control will increase from around 4 to 1 up to 20 to 1. This increased span of control will happen with the increased use of teams. Although this organizational structure will have areas of core competencies, it will be very fluid, constantly adjusting and learning. Andy Grove at Intel talks about constant reorganization and Mike Murray of Microsoft talks about their high velocity environment.

From Security to the new Covenant. The November 29, 1994 issue of the **Wall Street Journal** reported...

> **The social contract between employers and employees, in which companies promise to ensure employment and guide the careers of loyal troops, is dead, dead, dead.**

Organizations are moving from lifetime employment where the employer is responsible for careers to the new covenant of employment based on business needs and competencies. Hartford Insurance Company's Information Management organization has changed the psychological contract of their joining-up process to include a clear setting of expectations based upon the individual's responsibility for continual learning, keeping their competencies current, and being flexible and adjusting to change. Texas Instruments warns people, up to one year in advance of a change, that their job may not be there in the future, and help them retrain and look for a job inside and outside of TI. Thus, we are in the process of replacing the *organizational ethic*, which was based on hard work and security, with the *professional ethic*. The individual contributor with the professional ethic does not expect lifetime employment but is motivated by challenging work, rewards tied to performance, and is committed to the project and mission - not the organization.

People. In the past, organizations tended to hire and promote people who were alike in attitudes, values, and feelings. The organization of the future will value diversity and, with different inputs into the decision-making process, the quality of the decisions will be improved. The key to diversity is to have IT leaders who can *hear diverse opinions* and understand the value of different inputs to enhance competitive innovation.

Work Design. The traditional way or organizing work with job descriptions and specific responsibilities may become a social artifact that has outlived its usefulness.[10] Approximately 50 percent of a software engineer's productivity is the match-up of the person and the job. Therefore, creating meaningful work for IT people has tremendous potential to provide rich opportunities for increasing productivity and is one of the major areas overlooked by many IT organizations. The organization of the future will have broader jobs, more job rotation, more job enrichment, and people will move from project to project. All of these movements will result in increased job satisfaction. To qualify for the jobs of the future, people must alter their expectations from those of being dependent upon the employer to look after their best interests to one of constantly upgrading their skills and being flexible.

Motivation. Closely tied to work design is motivation. In the long run all human energy is volunteered and the STAR organization is designed to tap in on that energy which is intrinsic motivation. This concept is discussed in detail in Chapter 3.

Markets. There is a tremendous increase in world markets for the products of the business with the implementation of NAFTA and GATT. Global markets are a reality and global competition will increase in the 1990s. IT leaders will be held accountable to motivate people who design software and systems that support these markets.

Strategic Advantage. During the 1980s American corporations became enthralled with strategic planning, cutting costs, total quality management, and business process reengineering, and in many cases productivity did not improve. In the STAR organization, all of these management processes are important, but in addition to watching costs and implementing the latest management fad, IT leaders must deliver technology and services in a timely manner. The IT department at Reynolds & Reynolds found that filling an order for its business forms took 90 separate steps. They were able to reduce the steps to 20 and the time from quoting the order to shipment went from three weeks to one week.[11] The *fast cycle organization* will be first to market which will result in a sustained competitive advantage for the organization. The organization that can get its product to market first has a temporary monopoly and can price the product accordingly. In free enterprise, if the price is excessive, competition will enter the market place but by then the firm who was first to market has an established clientele, goodwill, and may be well into the second generation of product development. During periods of random change, time based competition will be the key to success. The larger companies are no longer dominating the market over the smaller companies, rather, the faster companies are out performing the slower companies!

Structure. The mature organization is based upon division of labor, job descriptions, and functions. For example, the typical management information systems organization was functionally divided into systems, technical services and operations. The organization of the future will be designed to support projects which are process driven. This movement has already started as evidenced by the large number of IT organizations implementing business process reengineering programs. A word of caution is in order here. Business process reengineering programs have a low success rate over the long run because the early "gurus" did not take into consideration the human side of information technology. Now even the early promoters of business process reengineering are speaking and writing about the need to develop commitment in the people. This methodology, to be effective, *must really be a planned change program.*

Quality. During the period of incremental change, quality was OK from the point of view of the manufacturing firms. The best example of this is the United States automotive industry. During the period of rapid change the quality programs were introduced into America by people such as Deming, Juran, and Crosby. Because of the lack of confidence in products manufactured in America, these quality programs became the latest quick-fix and America ended up with quality programs that had no compromises. An example was the zero defects program. By the end of the 1980s, leaders in the quality movement were beginning to realize it is not cost effective to drive every process or system to no defects. Further, they also began to speak about and build into their quality courses the need to implement effective change. Thus, in the early 1990s came the realization that there is a trade off between time to market and quality. This commitment to speed can lead software developers to push out products before they are fully tested. There are numerous examples of this problem in the software industry. Despite this trade off, time based competition will be the mantra of the 1990s!

Focus. While IT leaders must keep their eyes on budgets, the focus in the STAR organization is on the customer. The competencies of the future, in addition to superior technical skills, will be consulting, negotiation, and marketing skills. Some leaders in retooling their individual contributors are H-P, United Technologies Carrier, Citibank, and AT&T.

Guidelines for Creating the STAR Organization

In summary, our vision is that the STAR organization is the

structure that will best support the strategies of effective information technology organizations in periods of random change. We know of no organization that has all of the STAR values and competencies in place; however, some IT leaders are making tremendous progress in that direction. It is our thesis that the more of the values and variables of the STAR organization that are in place, the higher the probability the IT organization will be adding value to the bottom line.

The STAR organization is a high performance model that places strong emphasis on four bottom line factors. (1) High performance teams which work on process and quality products, (2) People feel valued. These *gold collar individual contributors* are highly competent, are motivated, and are change champions. (3) There is superior customer service - both external and internal. (4) There is a clear vision, core values, and strategic objectives which result in focus and alignment of the IT organization.[12]

We end this chapter with the guidelines for creating the STAR organization. Figure 1-5 contains the key steps that an IT leader must follow to position the organization to have a sustained competitive advantage in the 1990s. This is not a list to pick and choose from. These steps should be followed to insure a successful transformation of the mature IT organization.

1.	Steering committee	Establish a steering committee of key organizational movers.
2.	Team-building	Use team-building as an unfreezing process.
3.	Vision and values	Get buy in on the IT vision and STAR values and communicate to all individual contributors and customers.
4.	Strategic and tactical objectives	Establish strategic and tactical objectives & communicate to all individual contributors and customers.
5.	Define and assess core competencies	What competencies are critical to accomplish the objectives and do we have the right people?
6.	Organize around projects and processes	Create cross-functional teams around key projects that concentrate on process. Create a very flat organization with project leaders reporting to the IT director.
7.	Bureaucracy bashing	Assign a team to evaluate all activities and the value they add to the strategic objectives. Eliminate any activity, measurement, meeting, management layer, approval level that does not add value to the bottom line.
8.	Establish specific performance measures	Set performance measures for each project and process. Evaluate project leaders on their technical competencies and their ability to implement effective change.
9.	Benchmark	Dont reinvent the wheel. Have the steering committee visit other leading edge firms.
10.	Link rewards to STAR behavior	Establish a 360 degree performance appraisal, assessment center, and rewards that are team based.
11.	Institutionalize the change program	Many change programs do not last because more effort goes into planning and implementing rather than maintaining it.
12.	Communicate, communicate, and communicate	This cannot be overdone!

Figure 1-5. Guidelines for Creating the STAR Organization.

References

1. W. Rosser, "Rebuilding the IS Organization," **IS Research Note**, July 12, 1994, Gartner Group. page 1 and "Trendlines," **CIO**, April 1, 1995, page 14.

2. Ray Stata, "Organizational Learning - The Key to Management Innovation," **Sloan Management Review**, Spring, 1989, pp. 63-74.

3. Presentation by Mike Murray, Vice President Microsoft, 9th Annual Symposium for Human Resource Executives in I/S, October 13, 1994, Seattle.

4. Rob Thomsett, "The Clash of Two Cultures: Project Management Versus Process Management," **American Programmer**, June, 1994, pp. 18-28.

5. Please see Robert A. Zawacki and Carol A. Norman, "Successful Self-Directed Teams and Planned Change: A Lot in Common," in **Organization Development and Transformation: Managing Effective Change** (Burr Ridge, Ill: Irwin, 1994) 4th. ed., pp. 309-316., and Robert A. Zawacki and Carol A. Norman, "Managing Information Technology: From Incremental to Random Change," **Information Systems Management**, Summer, 1993, page 10.

6. This concept and Figure 1-1 are modifications of. Verne Morland, "Lear's Fool: Coping with Change beyond Future Shock," **New Management**, 2, no. 2 (1984).

7. Chris Argyris, "Teaching Smart People How to Learn," **Harvard Business Review**, May-June, 1991, pp. 99-109.

8. For a detailed discussion on the human consequences of moving from the mature organization to the STAR organization see Ronald E. LeBleu and Roger T. Sobkowiak, "Resolving Paradoxes of Change", **Information Systems Management**, Summer, 1993, pp. 7-12.

9. The content of Figure 1-2 was influenced by Jack K. Fordyce and Raymond Weil, **Managing with People** (Reading, MA.: Addison-Wesley Publishing Company, 1971) and David K.

Banner and T. Elaine Gagne, **Designing Effective Organizations** (Thousand Oaks, CA.: Sage Publications, 1995).

10. William Bridges, "The End of the Job," **Fortune**, September 19, 1994, pp. 62-74.

11. "Pushing the Pace," **Wall Street Journal**, December 12, 1994, page 1.

12. The definition of a high performance organization came from a conversation with Professor D. D. Warrick, College of Business and Administration, University of Colorado, Colorado Springs, Colorado, USA.

Chapter 2

Reenergizing People Before Reengineering

The real issue in the 90s is change management. Even the right things done the wrong way are unlikely to succeed. Change management can have far-reaching ramifications. An executive calls employees together for a one-hour meeting to announce a new reorganization that will solve most of the organization's problems. A year later, the organization is still in a state of chaos from the one-hour meeting. There was no commitment to the change . . . except by the executive. There was no involvement by the *key stakeholders* (those who are in the best position to influence and contribute to the success of the desired change) . . . The list goes on and on. Perhaps most alarming, the executive probably thinks everything is going well![1]

During the 1980s many information technology organizations reduced their headcount by numbers approaching 30 percent. After downsizing, some IT leaders told their remaining people that they were the "best of the very best" and the IT organization will move forward. Further, because they had to do more with less, the remaining people were told to be innovative and take risks. After the uncertainty of a reduction in force, the last thing the remaining people want to do is stick their necks out and take a risk. They are experiencing the feelings of guilt and fear. While experiencing guilt over the fact that their friends left, the remaining people also had a fear of the future.

Then some organizational leaders realized that they did not cut deep enough and had to have a second downsizing. As employee morale reached an all time low,[2] some IT leaders then attempted to increase productivity by implementing one of the many current change programs such as total quality management, self directed teams or business process reengineering. One computer manufacturing firm even had what the employees labeled as the *weekly Monday morning layoff*, while the managers were telling their employees they should be thankful for a job. Still other consultants talk about constitutional governance as the new way to manage information systems in the new era of decentralized companies. Too often IT leaders and managers don't stop and reflect on the challenges of change programs as the organization ventures forward after downsizing of their people.

From Fat to Muscle

It is our contention that many IT organizations are not cutting fat anymore, they are cutting muscle. Wherever we go in organizations, we observe that people are working longer hours and enjoying it less. In the short run, people can maintain their previous level of customer service and productivity by working longer and harder. In the long run, however, overwork will take its toll because we are cutting more than fat - we are cutting muscle. Further, IT leaders are not recognizing the need of their remaining people to grieve about the people who left and speculate about the future. Recently a division of a publicly traded Western United States computer manufacturing organization was purchased by a family and the new CEO asked all departments in the firm to downsize by forty percent. The customer service department was asked to reduce their headcount from ten to six people. After extensive tension and anxiety, the customer support supervisor made the reductions and told her remaining people of the need to put the cuts behind them and move forward as a team. Approximately six months later, the new owner told management that he did not cut deep enough to return to profitability and the customer support area was directed to go from six to two people. Again, after much soul searching, the customer support supervisor made the decision and she became a working supervisor with one other person. The two people are now doing the work of the previous ten, working 12 hours a day, and are even giving customer support over the telephone from their homes in the evening, and are facing ever increasing mounting job pressures. One of the remaining two people, who loves her work, is looking for another job only because she knows she cannot continue to work 12 hours a day, seven days a week and have any personal life.

Recently the **Wall Street Journal** (September 27, 1994) reported that a record 26 percent of companies polled plan to eliminate jobs again by June 30, 1995. This number will probably be much higher based on past experiences. In previous years, two to three times as many companies eliminated employees, compared to what they predicted. Alfred J. Dunlap, CEO of Scott Paper Company, says that repeated rounds of downsizings don't work. "If you keep doing (sizable job cuts), you destroy morale and you paralyze the company."

Although a reduction in force always introduces the twin emotions of fear and guilt in the remaining employees, John T. Crawford, Vice President of Information Management at The Hartford ITT, was the change champion for an innovative downsizing process in their information systems organization. They used a three part response to their reduction in staff in 1991. Their response was (1) to design a voluntary enhanced exit program, (2) a special assignment team was formed as a temporary home to further support information systems people whose positions were eliminated, and (3) a reorganization of the technical areas was set in motion. Through the effective management of the change process by the IT leaders, the information management department minimized the impact of this downsizing on productivity and even received favorable publicity in the local and national press.

Reenergizing People After Downsizing

Figure 2-1 depicts a journey that IT leaders should begin if they desire to create the STAR organization that will add value to the bottom line of their customers. Remember, *people add value to the customer when they feel valued.*[3]

After downsizing, the journey must begin with an off-site team building session where the leadership team has a voice in shaping the vision, values, strategic and tactical goals of the organization. After an off-site with the top leadership team, every leader must meet with their individual contributors and develop a process that increases their participation and buy-in to the vision, strategic, and tactical goals of the organization.

The importance of a clear vision and values cannot be overstated. A clear vision and values are the stakes in the ground that pull people toward the future when "turf" conflicts begin to surface during a planned change program. Many IT organizations have a vision and values that are not *owned* by the organizational members. Further, goals are extremely important at this stage of the journey. The remaining people are searching for focus and alignment because they have a high need for structure and goal clarity. After this off-site, the IT leader should appoint a team of about six people to benchmark with other IT organizations.

The benchmarking team should consist of about six people, three managers and three individual contributors, who are excellent communicators. Their task should be to visit other IT organizations to look at the *performance of key processes* such as systems development, new technology introduction, and operations. They should look for innovative human resource systems to support such high performance processes and the learning organization. Each team member should be assigned key learning objectives and then be prepared to share their learning outcomes with other team members and their IT organization. For example, 360 degree performance appraisal is a system to evaluate a team member with multiple evaluations from peers (team members), customers, the coach, and a self rating (see Chapter 5 for an in-depth discussion). Some firms using 360 degree performance appraisal, and possible benchmarking firms are Digital Equipment Corporation, Johnson and Johnson Advanced Behavioral Technology, Federal Express, and Ford Microelectronics.[4] While benchmarking, the team should also search for firms with innovative team-based compensation systems and true learning organizations because those are the systems and skills needed to survive in the 1990s.

Bureaucracy Bashing. After an off-site for team-building and extensive benchmarking, the next stop on the journey toward restoring trust is bureaucracy bashing. Bureaucracy bashing is basically reverse engineering or questioning every meeting, every level of approval for a decision, every report generated by information systems, and unnecessary measurements. This concept is similar to GE's workout sessions or Jaquar's egg groups. Some consulting companies refer to these sessions as a *quick strikes*. Figure 2-2 contains extensive guidelines for this critical process. Some IT leaders also use *quick hits* and *early wins* as tactical moves to begin the process of restoring trust in the organization. The basic objective of bureaucracy bashing is to remove low value work and create "headroom" for overworked employees while building trust.

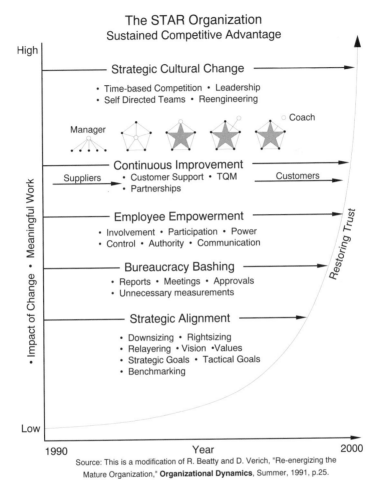

The STAR Organization
Sustained Competitive Advantage

Figure 2-1. Creating the IT Organization of the Future.

This step in creating the STAR organization is important because individual contributors are overworked after downsizing and their trust of any further management directed change programs is suspect at best. Therefore, appointing a team to eliminate unnecessary or low priority work will begin the process of empowering people and re-building trust with the IT leaders. Our experience is that IT leaders resist this step because they honestly believe that all of their systems, measurements, meetings, and approval levels are necessary, based on their institutional experiences (single-loop learning). The following examples illustrate this point and also give examples of how some IT leaders encourage double-loop learning in their organizations.

An information systems consultant was working with a major East coast financial institution and mentioned the need for bureaucracy bashing after their recent downsizing. Sitting in the front of the room with his back to the assistant vice presidents, was the senior vice president for information systems. When bureaucracy basing was suggested as a method to eliminate work and focus on priorities, he said, "We don't need any more team meetings on this topic, everything we do is necessary." The consultant said, "You should have seen the eyes of the assistant vice presidents roll back into their heads when they heard the comment!"

Another example, a senior vice president of a Southern utility company, asked all of his IT leadership team to go off-site and do reverse engineering. He started the meeting with the objectives for the day and then put up on a large flip chart every meeting he attended in the past week and asked each member of the leadership team, if they called the meeting, to justify the meeting. He also questioned every meeting that he scheduled. After eliminating or reducing unnecessary meetings that he attended during the past week, he then asked each of his direct reports to list all of their meetings in the previous week and anyone in the room could comment on the purpose, length of, and real need for the meeting.

One Eastern insurance company used bureaucracy bashing to reinforce the idea of empowerment in their information systems organization. The CIO tasked a team of eight systems analysts to question every report, measurement, approval level, and meeting within the 400 person development area. Further, he announced the assignment at a leadership meeting and had the bureaucracy bashing team give a progress report to the leadership team each month. Thus, he gave high visibility to the bureaucracy bashing team while keeping the leadership team in the communication loop. As the team brought forth suggestions, the CIO implemented some ideas immediately (quick strikes) to reinforce the idea of speed and the importance of the project. Where there were more complicated issues that involved the customers or technology, he publicly assigned the recommendation to an action committee for evaluation with a clear deadline for them to report back to the leadership team. Although the IT organization had previously stated that they were moving away from a paternalistic organization, through this bureaucracy bashing process, individual contributors began to understand what empowerment is and that their IT leaders were committed to changing the organizational culture toward a learning organization.

Empowerment of People

Empowerment is the current *catch phrase* or *buzz word*. In many of our consulting engagements, our customers ask us to define this buzz word. A standard definition of empowerment is **pushing decision rights down in the organization to where the expert or local knowledge is based. Succinctly it matches the decision maker with the one who has the best knowledge for that decision.** We could continue to write about sharing of power with individual contributors, two way communication, and authority that is based on expert knowledge rather than position authority; however, we prefer to define it in behavioral terms. Many IT leaders can talk the talk but their behavior soon gives them away because in an emergency or crisis they tend to revert to their old autocratic top down style. True IT leaders understand the power of committed people.

Trying to define employee empowerment is similar to the difficulty of defining pornography. Its dilemma was best summed up in former Justice Potter Stewart's now famous statement: "I shall not today attempt to define (obscenity); and perhaps I could never succeed in intelligibly doing so. But I know it when I see it." We define empowerment by observing leadership behavior in IT organizations.

When a crisis appears, it is easy for IT leaders to fall into the trap of reverting to their old leadership style of control and problem-solving behavior because that is what they were taught in MBA programs and solving problems is rewarding to their psyche. They thrive on crisis management.

Recently a major aircraft manufacturing company designed around self directed teams, a very flat organization that told their employees they were empowered to make decisions affecting the

1. Ask for 10-12 volunteers to serve on a *bureaucracy bashing team*.

2. The majority of the volunteers should be individual contributors - not managers.

3. Dedicate one day a week, or more, that the team works on bureaucracy bashing.

4. Have the team report directly to the top information systems director.

5. The senior information systems person should meet personally with the team and give them the charge!

6. Communicate the objectives and importance of the team to all organizational members.

7. After the charge, explain to the team what bureaucracy bashing is all about and ask them to:
   a. Log every meeting they will attend during the next week (length, who called the meeting, agenda, etc.).
   b. Ask one team member to research the approval levels and process for a trip to a typical professional meeting and the reimbursement process.
   c. Other team members are assigned an existing measurement tool, then they are to research the steps, processes and time required to do the measurement.
   d. Each team member comes to the next meeting with a list of reports within information systems and between information systems and their customers that can be eliminated.

8. The team continues to meet weekly to question every report, meeting, approval level, and measurement.

9. The bureaucracy bashing team briefs the top IT leadership team every month. This briefing reinforces the importance of the process, sets expectations, and permits the bureaucracy bashing team to make adjustments to leadership input, if necessary.

10. After the team makes its final recommendations, a steering committee is asked to review all recommendations and plan for the implementation of the agreed upon recommendations.

11. Communicate the final recommendations to all IT members.

12. Consider recognition and a reward for the team members.

Figure 2-2. Guidelines for Bureaucracy Bashing.

value added to the bottom line, had an emergency at 4:30 p.m. on the Friday afternoon prior to the Labor Day three day weekend. The leadership team of six people (all with MBAs) immediately called a meeting and began working the issue. After 2 hours of flow charts, a diagram of the critical path, talk of hiring part time workers and even flying in additional help, and a general good feeling by the leadership team that they were on top of the issue, one of the leadership team said, "What are we doing? If we truly empowered our self directed teams, they should be in here working this issue."

When the leadership team realized the importance of this challenge, they called the team back to the plant, gave the problem to them and said they would be at home if they were needed. The self directed team designed a strategy to solve the problem, scheduled themselves to work all of the three day weekend, and when the manufacturing technicians arrived on Tuesday morning, the system was up and running. That demonstrates the commitment of empowered people who feel valued and trusted!

One important warning on empowerment - there are some risks and downsides to empowering people in certain jobs. For example, imagine if all of the London underground train conductors were empowered to make decisions on their schedules! IT leaders should examine their routine and rote job types with the objective of still requiring top down control structures for those jobs.

Continuous Improvement Based on Trust

The Japanese call it *kaizen*, which means "change in small doses." A recent study by the American Quality Foundation[5] shows that most total quality programs are a bust because TQM programs tried to implement 9000 new practices simultaneously. Their conclusions were: (1) involve everyone in the change process, and (2) be willing to change everything but concentrate on one thing at a time.

In addition to the above conclusions, we believe that most continuous improvement and partnering programs are failing because individual contributors are overworked, lack alignment, and feel de-valued by their leaders. Further, forming a successful partnership program with suppliers and customers is a long term complex change program that must be managed from the top (see Figure 2-3). When the impact and complexity of the change program is low, the program can be managed effectively by a first level

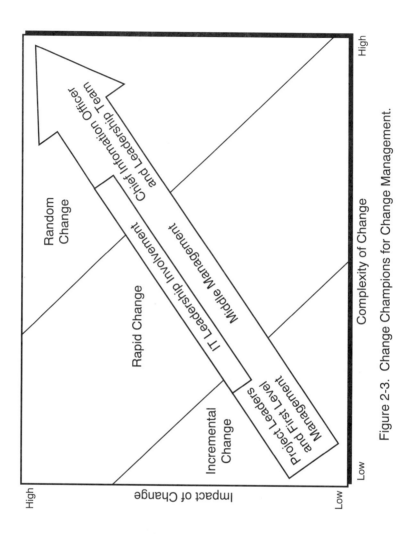

Figure 2-3. Change Champions for Change Management.

manager. However, as complexity and the impact of the change increase, the involvement of IT leaders must move up to middle management or even the CIO. A total quality management program definitely has high organizational impact and complexity.

In our opinion, the error many IT leaders made in the 1990s in their rush to embrace the total quality movement was that although they recognized the importance of quality they put more effort into planning than they did into implementation and follow-up. During periods of *random change* top IT leaders must be the change champions for major initiatives such as total quality management.

Arriving at Strategic Cultural Change

If strategic alignment, bureaucracy bashing, empowerment, and continuous improvement, are implemented properly by IT leaders, then individual contributors will feel valued. People who feel valued add value to the organization and the customer. Also, there is a higher probability of self directed teams or business process reengineering efforts being successful because there is a minimum level of trust between all organizational members that is a necessary foundation for these change processes. When these change processes are in place, then the IT organization will have a sustained competitive advantage and will have a high probability of becoming a STAR organization.

The final stage of renewal is really an outgrowth of the other four. Fundamental cultural change means that employees' mindset - the way they think about their work is shifted. Employees do not feel part of a "mature" company, but they see themselves as having faced and overcome the renewal change challenge. They feel the enthusiasm and commitment of trying new approaches to work and, as a result, they bring more desirable changes into the organization.[6]

Test Your Assumptions About Your IT Organization

You may be reading this dissertation about moving from the mature organization to the STAR organization and feel that your IT organization is well on the journey to becoming the organization of the future. Test your assumptions! Ask six managers to complete Figure 2-4 and return the unsigned survey to you. Then ask six to ten software engineers or systems analysts to complete the survey. Average each group and compare the results. Do you have a difference in perceptions between the managers and the individual contributors? If your people rate their IT organization a score of 51 or higher you are indeed very close to or actually a STAR organization. Congratulations!

However, if both groups rate the organization as a 50 or lower, your IT organization needs help. Further, if your individual contributors give the organization a score of 50 or lower and the managers give the organization a score of 51 or better, this is an indication that the organization lacks alignment and the IT leadership needs to work harder at developing a mindset where people feel valued and add value to the bottom line of the customer.

Also, notice that the meaningfulness of work for the individual contributor increases as the IT organization continues the journey of creating the STAR organization. Because providing meaningful work for people who want to achieve is the key to motivation, we examine this match-up between work and people in depth in Chapter 3.

How Competitive is Your IT Organization? Many IT organizations have downsized in recent years as much as thirty percent, yet a simple reduction in staff (headcount) does not always make for a lean organization. For an IT organization to be flexible, flat, and constantly learning, there are key company characteristics that indicate if the organization is capable of maintaining a culture that produces a sustained competitive advantage. Using the scale below, rate your IT organization on each characteristic with 1 being low and 7 being very high. Then total your score and compare it to the averages in the table below.

Circle the response that best describes your IT organization.

1. To what extent do we keep the customer happy?

   1   2   3   4   5   6   7

   Keep the boss happy; only talk about the customer.

   Keep the customer happy; they pay our bills.

2. How committed is this IT organization to innovation and new ideas?

   1   2   3   4   5   6   7

   Don't make waves; keep our heads down.

   We make waves which result in innovation.

3. How open is communication in this IT organization?

   1   2   3   4   5   6   7

   Communication is very guarded and closed.

   Excellent communication in all directions.

4. Do people feel valued in this IT organization?

   1   2   3   4   5   6   7

   People feel devalued.

   People feel very valued.

Figure 2-4. Reenergizing the IT Organization: Moving Toward the Organization of the Future (STAR).

5. How are problems handled?

1	2	3	4	5	6	7

If something goes wrong,
blame someone else.

The buck stops here. We accept
ownership of the problems and
get them solved.

6. How many layers of people are there from the CEO to an entry level
   programmer?

1	2	3	4	5	6	7

13 or more.   7 to 9.   Less than 5 layers.

7. Number of individual contributors managed or coached by a typical
   supervisor?

1	2	3	4	5	6	7

3 or less.   7 to 9.   More than 20.

8. What is the skills level of your management group?
   (Skills includes technical and people)

1	2	3	4	5	6	7

Low   Average   High

9. Is this IT organization a learning organization?
   (We have the capacity to act, reflect on our decision, and learn
   from our mistakes)

1	2	3	4	5	6	7

Tomorrow will be
just like today.

Nobody knows what tomorrow
will bring. Constant learning to
prepare for the future.

Figure 2-4 continued. Reenergizing the IT Organization: Moving Toward
the Organization of the Future (STAR).

10. How much collaboration is there in this IT organization?

1	2	3	4	5	6	7

People compete when they
need to cooperate. They are
jealous of their area of
responsibility.

Collaboration is freely entered
into. Ways of helping others
is widely developed.

SCORING INSTRUCTIONS

Total your score and check the block below:

_____ 10 through 30 points - We need help now!
_____ 31 through 50 points - Just getting by - not to worry!
_____ 51 through 60 points - Approaching excellence!
_____ 61 or more points - A true learning (STAR) organization!

After totaling your individual score, break into groups of approximately 10
people and have a group discussion on each question. One approach is to ask
the two people who rated that dimension the lowest and highest to share their
views with the group.

Figure 2-4 continued. Reenergizing the IT Organization: Moving Toward
the Organization of the Future (STAR).

References

1. D. D. Warrick, "What Executives, Managers, and Human Resource Professionals Need to Know About Managing Change," in Wendell L. French, Cecil H. Bell, Jr., and Robert A. Zawacki, **Organization Development and Transformation: Managing Effective Change** (Burr Ridge, Ill.: Irwin, 1994), pp. 463-472.

2. General satisfaction of systems people decreased from 5.29 (on a scale of 1 to 7 with 7 high) in 1979 to 4.80 in 1993. See Robert A. Zawacki, "Motivating IT People in the 90s: An Alarming Drop in Job Satisfaction," **The Software Practitioner**, November- December, 1993, pp. 1-5.

3. The January 30, 1995 issue of **Business Week,** page 6, contains a review, by John A. Byrne, of the book by Champy **Reengineering Management.** The reviewer writes that Champy now admits reengineering did not live up to its expectations because the key problem is management itself. Thus, his new book. Then the reviewer goes on to say that the book contains . . ."an exasperating flaw . . . no one speaks to the first and perhaps most agonizing and divisive process - mobilizing employees to accept the changes reengineering entails." We highlight this review because we believe that our concept of *people must feel valued before they add value to the customer* begins to address the concerns of the **Business Week** reviewer. Further, through the process of bureaucracy bashing, the people in the organization begin to rebuild trust and begin the slow journey toward accepting change. This process of reenergizing people through participation makes them feel valued and begins the process of re-establishing trust!

4. John F. Milliman, Robert A. Zawacki, Carol Norman, Lynda Powell and Jay Kirksey, "Companies Evaluate Employees From All Perspectives," **Personnel Journal**, November, 1994, pp. 99-103. Another source for benchmarking is the **Annual Symposium for Human Resource Executives in Information Systems** which is a network of sixty I/S executives. For information on this Symposium please call 719 599-0849.

5.   Gilbert Fuchsberg, "Quality Programs Show Shoddy Results," **Wall Street Journal**, May 14, 1992, page 1.

6.   R. Beatty and D. Verich, "Re-energizing the Mature Organization," **Organizational Dynamics**, Summer, 1991, page 28.

Chapter 3

Motivating Information Technology People to Increased Productivity

Introduction

Seventeen years have passed since our landmark study[1] on what motivates programmers, programmers/analysts, analysts, technical services, operations, and information systems managers. We continue to update the original research[2] and have expanded the research into Europe, the Far East, Australia, and Scandinavian countries. Does the same motivational model apply for research and managing people in the 1990s that was used as the basis for our original research in the 1970s and 1980s?

Definition of Motivation

Before we can answer this question, we need to have a general understanding of the term "motivation."[3] Supervisors, coaches, leaders, parents and teachers are constantly charged with the responsibility of motivating other people. In theory, that sounds like a worthwhile goal, but in practice it is difficult to accomplish because of the elusive nature of the word "motivation."

Motivation is difficult to discuss because it cannot be seen, felt, heard, tasted or smelled. It is something that simply exists in our language and culture, and researchers have labeled those things "concepts." Because each of us defines concepts based on how we have experienced the world (conditioning), a diagram of the concept of motivation maybe a helpful starting point toward a definition.

Needs and Tension Begin the Motivation Process. Motivation theory has been called need theory. Human beings begin the behavior process with a felt need that produces tension with their systems. This tension may be the need for food, sex, power, human interaction, achievement, or even some object such as a home or car. Using the example of a car, people may feel the need for a new car because: (1) they ride the bus to work while everyone

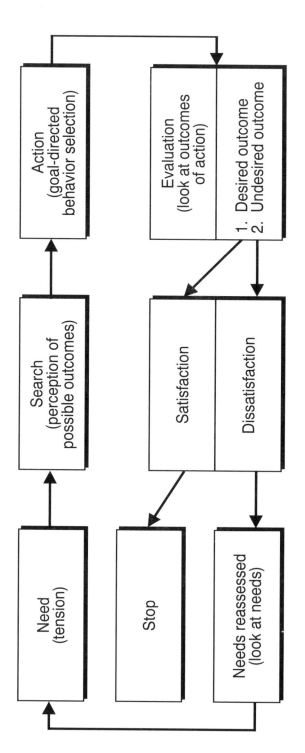

Figure 3-1. The Motivation Concept.

else drives a personal automobile, (2) their present car is in need of expensive repairs and has high mileage, or (3) a new car may be viewed by them as a status symbol to impress their friends.

We Search the Environment. Once aware of the need (tension), people begin a search process for ways of satisfying the need. In the car example, the person with the want can visit a number of new car showrooms and make some comparisons. They may compare Fords, Buicks, BMWs, and Hondas. During the search process, each person ranks the cars according to their perceptions of how each car will meet their perceived needs. Please remember that a motivator must be perceived as a motivator by the person with the need before it is truly a motivator of behavior. All too often, leaders and supervisors believe they know what motivates their individual contributors when, in fact, the leader's perception is different from the individual contributor's perception.

The search process can vary from the simple, such as, where will a person go to lunch, to the complex end of the search process which is artificial intelligence. In artificial intelligence the researchers are actually attempting to duplicate the human decision making process on a software program.

People Take Action. After searching for solutions for our need, we rank the cars according to our subjectively calculated probability of each car's ability to satisfy our need. Then we purchase (select) the car with the highest probability. For example, we may want a car that delivers over 30 miles per gallon of gas, is comfortable to drive, and is viewed as above average on status by our friends. Subjectively, the buyer ranks this purchase above a vacation, CD player or some other purchase.

Evaluation of the Choice. After purchasing a certain car - a Volvo, for example - the new owners constantly evaluate the car to see if it meets their expectations. In the evaluation process the owners look at the mileage, repair costs, warranty, and comfort of the car and again subjectively compare it to the performance of other makes of cars. Now a unique process may take place in the owners' minds if they begin to believe that the Volvo does not meet their expectations. This process is known as ***cognitive dissonance***.[4] Because the state of cognitive dissonance is uncomfortable to the purchasers, they will attempt to reduce the dissonance and achieve more balance in their minds by doing one of five things:

1. The purchasers can ignore the new inputs that do not agree with their original expectations.

2. The purchasers can recognize the new inputs but rationalize the accuracy of the new inputs. For example, "I am only getting 23 miles per gallon of gas but almost all of my driving is in the city."

3. The purchasers can blame themselves. ("We did not check into mileage before we made the decision.")

4. The purchasers can blame someone else. ("The salesperson did not give us accurate information on gas mileage.")

5. The purchasers can accept the inputs as accurate and regret the purchase. ("We really didn't want a Volvo anyway.")

These five techniques are methods of coping with uncomfortable perceptions that the purchasers may have.

Satisfaction or Dissatisfaction. After driving the new car, the purchasers may experience satisfaction or dissatisfaction. For example, if the purchasers ignore inputs that do not agree with their expectations, they may be satisfied and the original need (a new car) is fulfilled. A satisfied (fulfilled) need is no longer a motivator because the tension or desire no longer exists. Further, it is the searching process for a new car that is a motivator, once the need is meet, it (the car) is no longer a motivator.

Reevaluate the Alternatives. If the evaluation of the car results in dissatisfaction, the purchasers may again evaluate other cars that will satisfy their needs. Thus, the state of dissatisfaction results in tension which may still be a motivator of behavior. Whether or not the people purchase another car will depend upon the strength of the need.

Basic Assumptions of Motivation. Linked to the definition of motivation are three basic assumptions: (1) human behavior is caused by a need, (2) human behavior is goal-oriented, and (3) human behavior is motivated.

Theories of Motivation

After exposing you to a brief definition of motivation, we will now introduce two main theories of motivation. Although there are many theories of motivation, we believe that most leaders or coaches will only remember a few theories and that is fine! Why even discuss any theories? A good theory of motivation is a "road map" for IT leaders to help them understand what is going on inside a programmer's mind.

Motivation-Hygiene Theory

The first theory of motivation we will discuss is generally referred to as *two factor theory* and it was presented in the 1950s by Frederick Herzberg.[5] Before Herzberg conceptualized his Motivation-Hygiene Theory, the assumption behind management training was that workers were dissatisfied. It was managements' job to determine why they were dissatisfied, and if possible meet their needs so the workers would be satisfied. It was further assumed that happy workers would be productive workers (see Figure 3-2).

Herzberg was the first person to say that dissatisfaction and satisfaction are not the end points of a continuous line. He advocated that without certain things at the place of work, workers will be dissatisfied. However, if a manager meets the workers' maintenance (hygiene) needs, they will not be satisfied; they only will be not dissatisfied or not unhappy. Thus, the workers move only half way on the top line in Figure 3-2. To be happy or satisfied, workers need jobs that basically have motivational characteristics or satisfiers.

Without the maintenance factors, workers will be unhappy; but given the maintenance factors they will not necessarily be happy. To motivate people to increased productivity, leaders must examine the satisfiers of a job after meeting employee maintenance needs. Also, the maintenance factors are concerned with the surroundings of the job (extrinsic or external factors), while the motivators are concerned with the job itself and how employees feel about their job (intrinsic or internal factors). Dr. Herzberg

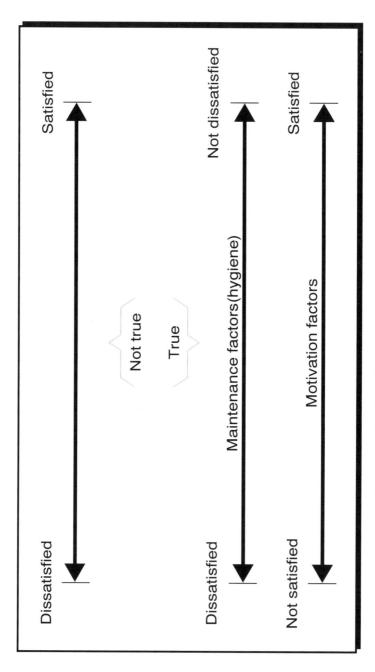

Figure 3-2. Satisfaction and Dissatisfaction.

was the first person to give management an actual list that they can use to motivate people. His list is:

Maintenance Factors (Hygiene)	**Motivation Factors (Satisfiers)**
Company policies	The work itself
Work conditions	Achievement
Supervision	Advancement and growth
Job security	Responsibility
Pay	Recognition
Interpersonal relations with co-workers	

It may be helpful to think of Motivation-Hygiene Theory as a house. The foundation is the hygiene factors and the house on top of the foundation is the motivators. Thus, if there is a crack in the foundation, it does not motivate people to talk about designing meaningful work until the foundation is fixed. An example is the current movement toward reducing head count. Most IT firms have downsized thirty percent, and then they tell the remaining people that they are "the chosen ones" and the firm will move forward. Although downsizing was probably necessary for survival, the security contract with the people has been broken and trust is low. Thus, there is a crack in the foundation. Many firms at this point implement a reengineering or total quality management program and it is doomed to failure because the people are not interested in making work more meaningful (a motivator). They are only interested in their survival (hygiene) and are probably wondering when the next layoff will come and who will be affected. When the foundation is again solid, then the leaders in the IT organization can begin to plan for an effective change program such as reengineering, CASE, TQM, or self directed teams.

Pay is listed as a dissatisfier, and this may puzzle the reader because everyone is willing to accept more pay. No one turns down a pay increase. Herzberg listed pay as a hygiene factor because his research indicated that when salary was perceived by the workers as unfair or inequitable, their negative feelings were three times as strong as when pay was considered fair. Thus, when pay scales are out of balance, workers are very dissatisfied; when they are in balance workers are only slightly happy.

In today's business climate of cost cutting and low salary increases (many are only keeping up with inflation), it is our contention that systems development and operations people view salary as a motivator. Further, our research indicates that many systems development people view salary as recognition for a job well done. Thus, a current comparative salary survey, shared with the people, is a must for the IT firm that is concerned about establishing trust and motivating people. Also, when recent college graduates are hired in a firm as entry level programmers, money is definitely a motivator. However, as they progress up the career ladder, money may move down on their priority list and the meaningfulness of work may move up to become their top priority.

Core Job Theory

Core Job Theory[6] is helpful to information systems leaders to create conditions for individual contributors' internal (intrinsic) motivation by providing meaningful work. If the job itself is motivational then leaders and managers can use their scarce time and resources to develop better customer service and concentrate more on other issues such as budgets and career development.

Core Job Theory can be viewed as an extension of Herzberg's Two Factor Theory because the core job dimensions are an extension of *the work itself* in Motivation-Hygiene Theory. Also, Core Job Theory is a true paradigm shift in the evolution of motivation research. Prior to core job theory, the underlying assumption of all motivation theories was to make individual contributors happy and then they will produce. Unfortunately, we went too far in America and ended up with a lot of happy people in the 1970s that were not productive! Many are still on our college campuses today.

Assumption Underlying Core Job Theory. When we started our original motivational research in the 1970s, we went to organizations (such as IBM, U.S. Labor Department, various states, Mutual of Omaha, H-P, and Hawaiian Airlines) and asked systems, operations, and technical services people what motivated them. Our objective was to establish a research hypothesis to guide our investigation of the human side of IT (in those days it was called DP). They never replied once that their working condi-

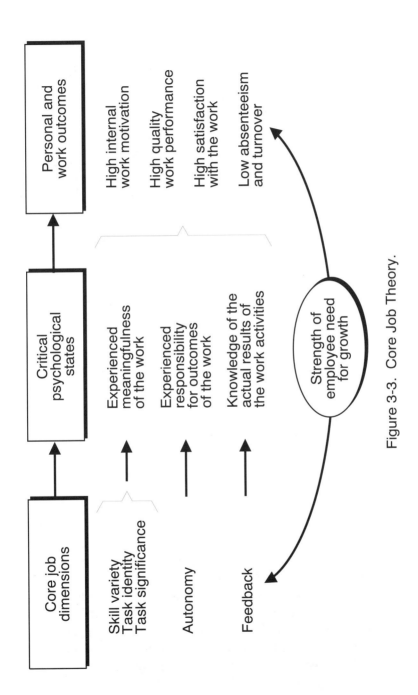

Figure 3-3. Core Job Theory.

tions, benefits, job security, or company policies motivated them. What they kept saying in various ways was they had exciting meaningful work! This finding fit a pattern that was just beginning to be discussed by researchers on motivation: the idea that productivity may lead to satisfaction. Thus, we continued our motivation research on the following paradigm shift:

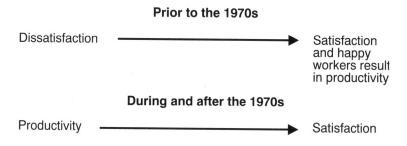

Prior to the 1970s

Dissatisfaction ⟶ Satisfaction and happy workers result in productivity

During and after the 1970s

Productivity ⟶ Satisfaction

Core Job Theory is based on the assumption that productivity leads to satisfaction. Thus, provide systems people with meaningful work, establish goals with deadlines, and if I/S management properly trained them, get out of the way (autonomy) and when they complete the goal on time they will feel good (job satisfaction)! The theory is based on the assumption that the five core job dimensions develop critical psychological states within the individual doing the work. Critical psychological states are their attitudes toward work which result in personal outcomes and organizational outcomes. Personal outcomes are visibility, recognition, opportunity for achievement, salary, and benefits. The organizational outcomes are high quality work, on time delivery, high productivity, and lower turnover.

An motivational example of the outcomes of core job theory is a software engineer developing software at Microsoft. That person working on developing the next version of Windows has a high presence of the five core job dimensions, which results in a very positive attitude toward the job (intrinsic motivation), which in turn results in high personal outcomes for the software engineer and high work outcomes for Microsoft. Bill Gates commented on the importance of meaningful work when he told the **Wall Street Journal** (November 8, 1994) ". . . we're supposed to make a person's job interesting and we're supposed to move them around to give them exposure to new things."

The reverse also holds true. Give people less than meaningful work and they develop a less than positive attitude toward work and the organizational outcomes and personal outcomes are lower. An example of this is in systems development after an application is designed and installed. Many customers ask that the same people who developed the system also remain on the project and maintain the system. Our research indicates that the meaningfulness of work decreases as the information systems development people move to maintenance. In Chapter 5 we will discuss how the coach or supervisor can increase the meaningfulness of work, such as maintenance, by simply increasing feedback.

Definition of the Five Core Job Dimensions. Meaningful jobs, those that challenge and stretch employees, are designed by concentrating on the five core job dimensions, which are combined to produce a motivating potential score (MPS). MPS is on a scale of 1 to 7 in which 7 is high or rich. Enhancing any of the five core job dimensions will increase a job's MPS. Obviously, the more of the core job dimensions that can be increased, the more the person doing the work will perceive the job as meaningful or rich. These five dimensions are:

1. **Skill Variety:** The degree to which a job requires a variety of different activities which in turn involves the use of a number of different skills and talents of the individual contributor. Examples of skill variety are job rotation, job enrichment, and training in new technology.

2. **Task Identity:** The degree to which the job requires the completion of a "whole" and identifiable piece of work - e. g., doing a job from beginning to end with a visible outcome. Also, structuring the work so the programmer can interact with the business organization will increase task identity.

3. **Task Significance:** The degree to which the job has a substantial impact on the lives or work of other people, whether in the immediate IT organization or with customers and clients.

4. **Autonomy:** The degree to which the job provides substantial freedom, independence, and discretion to the individual con-

tributors in scheduling their work and determining the procedures to be used in carrying it out. This does not mean the manager should say, "Do your best" or be a warm friendly helper. Rather, our research indicates that individual contributors want managers who help them define goals, measures of effectiveness, resources, deadlines, and then give them freedom to accomplish the goal.

5. **Feedback:** The degree to which carrying out the work activities required by the job results in employees obtaining information about the effectiveness of their performance. If the job itself does not provide enough feedback, then coaches or managers must provide the additional feedback.

Matching Jobs and People. High MPS jobs (such as development) should be assigned to people who thrive on being challenged, are stimulated by new technology, and developing their competencies beyond where they are. People who like being challenged are called high achievers and Core Job Theory labels them as high in growth need strength (GNS). Thus, MPS is an organizational variable and it can be increased by the manager or individual contributors "tweaking" the five core job dimensions. GNS is an individual variable which is the need for achievement that a person brings with them to the job. The objective is to match people and jobs. Our research indicates that approximately fifty percent of a programmer's productivity comes from this match-up. Give people high MPS jobs and they work too much. Give people lower MPS jobs and they work to a lesser degree of quality and productivity.

The GNS of people is set relatively early in life (usually around the time they are six to nine years old) and remains relatively firm for the remainder of their life. We formed focus groups with managers who hired high achievers and asked them to identify the traits they looked for in the joining-up process. The traits of high GNS people are: high goal orientation, very ambitious, very systematic, seeks out further education/training, inner directed, highly confident, high need for recognition, very assertive, highly inquisitive and has an excellent perspective to separate the unimportant from the very important. Our research on high GNS people further supports Core Job Theory which emphasizes the importance of high MPS jobs.

Research on the Motivation of IT People

Original Research. Our original research on the motivation of IT people in the 1970s was based on Core Job Theory. The instrument used to measure the match-up of the job and the individual was the Job Diagnostic Survey developed by J. Richard Hackman and Greg R. Oldham. We modified the instrument to include questions of such topics as access to the computer, access to technical help, goal setting, feedback on goal accomplishment and the amount of time the programmer/analyst spends on maintenance of existing systems. We labeled our modified instrument the **Job Diagnostic Survey - Information Technology (JDS-IT).** The JDS-IT has 77 questions, is answered anonymously, and takes about 30 minutes to complete. The instrument measures 28 variables on the human side of IT, which is 55% of the typical budget, and we report the results back by job and department or project. The results are then compared against our international norms which exist for 36 jobs in over 200 companies worldwide.[7]

Two of the major findings of this original research were: (1) information systems people had (on a scale of 1 to 7) the highest growth need strength (5.91) and, (2) the lowest social needs strength (4.20) in the 500 jobs measured in the original research. MPS and GNS were defined earlier. Social need strength (SNS) is a measure of a person's need to have meaningful interpersonal relationships with other people both on and off the job. It is a measure of need for affiliation.

A third major finding reported in 1979 was that information systems people received very poor feedback from their supervisors. Feedback was 3.97 on a scale of 1 being low and 7 being high. When compared to other professions this was an alarmingly low score. Further, feedback is the most important core job dimension and one of the easiest variables for supervisors to correct if they are interested in their subordinates' welfare. When we reported the results of our original research to user groups or in-house at various firms, most I/S people would say, "That high GNS is me but that low SNS is not me, but it is everyone else in my DP organization." Also, our research indicated that low SNS people are poor at giving feedback because they just are not as comfortable with the human side of managing.

Based on our research findings, many firms revised their selection process to hire high GNS and high SNS people because higher SNS people can learn feedback skills quicker and are more inclined to give good feedback. However, the majority of firms have to deal with high GNS and low SNS. One of our research findings concluded that if firms selected the best technical managers (with this personality profile) and provided them with an intensive course in giving and receiving feedback, those technical managers could do very well at giving feedback. Thus, if the firm made giving feedback a goal and evaluated the technical manager on how well they accomplished that goal, the managers became good at giving feedback. The key to changing behavior is to play to the technical manager's high GNS (goal oriented) and they will give good feedback if they know they will be measured on how they give feedback.

Updated Research. Figure 3-4 below is an update of our 1979 research. The GNS of the sampled international population has remained relatively stable over time. This is good because with the rapid technological change in IT we want people who are not threatened by new things. As a matter of fact, high GNS people thrive on learning new things.

Variable	1979	1995
Growth Need Strength (GNS) for all systems people	5.91	5.95
Motivating Potential Score (MPS)	5.35	5.42
Social Need Strength (SNS)	4.20	4.20
Feedback from Supervisors	3.97	4.19
General Satisfaction	5.29	4.80
Core competencies	Only Technical	Technical & People

Figure 3-4. Comparison of Major Motivation Research Variables 1979 to 1995.

The MPS of the job did not change significantly from 1979 to 1995. Thus, one of our major findings in 1979 still applies today. IT leaders must design strategies to increase the MPS of the job. The difference between 5.95 (GNS) and 5.42 (MPS) is the potential for increasing motivation and productivity or to put it another way, the difference of .53 is the untapped potential of the systems person doing the job. Remember, any of the five core job dimensions can be increased which will be perceived by the person doing the job as an improvement in the meaningfulness of work. The more of the core job dimensions that are changed, the higher the probability that the MPS of the job will be increased. Our research indicates that IT people almost always overhire for the job.[8] They select very high GNS people and then place them in jobs with lower MPS.

Social Needs Strength (SNS) did not change from 1979 to 1995. This trend indicates a problem within the I/S industry because the competencies have changed from primarily a technical focus to one of technical and people skills. An example is the movement of systems people into the business units. People with higher SNS have a need for more human interaction; also they are more motivated to learn change skills, negotiation skills and conflict resolution skills. This research finding indicates the need to select people with higher SNS and to train our present systems development people to be better at implementing change.

Although slightly higher than our 1979 findings, feedback from supervisors is still a problem. The I/S industry tends to take the best technical person and make them the manager or coach. When they are promoted, they take their low SNS with them which results in very low feedback to their direct reports and the customers. A high GNS and low SNS person will do the technical things first because solving technical problems is a motivator for them. Further, to give both positive and negative feedback is not natural with their low SNS. This does not mean that new systems managers cannot give good feedback; rather, this means that they must receive training on feedback skills. Giving good feedback is a learned skill. With today's camcorders used as a training tool, IT training managers should design and implement a two day course on good feedback skills for all new supervisors. When it is not possible to have a feedback course, we then recommend our Feedback Checklist which is included as Figure 3-5 at the end of this Chapter. Although not as good as a course, this checklist is an excellent first step toward helping technical managers give better feedback.

General Satisfaction. The alarming drop in general satisfac-

Name of individual contributor _____

Date _____

Directions

Personnel research indicates that high achievers (high GNS people) desire and need good feedback. Goals and feedback are the most critical dimensions of meaningful work. This form is designed to improve the quality of feedback between managers and individual contributors.

     First, the individual contributor answers the following questions by circling one of the numbers in each of the scales.

     Second, the manager of the individual contributor answers the questions, without seeing the individual contributor's responses.

     Third, they schedule a one hour meeting, in which the individual contributor and manager compare their answers on each dimension. Questions with more than a two point spread between answers are potential problem areas. The individual contributor's motivation and productivity can be increased if both parties jointly develop an action plan to improve those items with more than a two point spread.

1. How clear and specific are the goals for your job? That is, do you know the specific goals you are expected to accomplish?

1	2	3	4	5	6	7

Not very clear; I do not know what the goals are.	Somewhat clear; although the goals are not specific, I think I know what the goals are.	Very clear; I know exactly what the goals are.

2. To what extent do you have influence in the determination of your work objectives or goals?

1	2	3	4	5	6	7

Very little; I have little to say in determining my goals.	Moderately; I have some influence in determining my goals.	Very much; I have a great deal of influence in determining my goals.

Figure 3-5. Feedback Checklist.

tion from 5.29 (1979) to 4.80 (1995) should concern the I/S profession. We were very concerned with this finding and accomplished extensive focus groups to get a more in-depth understanding of this drop off. Programmers, programmer/analysts, and senior analysts in the focus groups all talked about:

3. How much feedback and guidence do you receive concerning the quantity and quality of your work goals?

1	2	3	4	5	6	7

Very little; I receive almost no feedback concerning my goals.

Moderate feedback.

Very much; I receive constant feedback concerning my goals.

4. To what extent does your manager let you know how well you are doing your job?

1	2	3	4	5	6	7

Very little; my manager almost never lets me know how well I am doing.

Moderately; sometimes my manager may give me feedback, other times he or she may not.

Very much; my manager provides me with almost constant feedback about how well I am doing.

5. To what extent does your manager let you in on the "big picture"? For example, if you are working on a subsystem, does your manager help you understand how your project fits into the total system?

1	2	3	4	5	6	7

Very little.

Moderately.

Always.

6. To what extent does your manager give you general feedback? For example, if you ask a question or request a short course, does your manager get back with you in a reasonable time frame?

1	2	3	4	5	6	7

Very little.

Moderately.

Always.

7. The amount of support and guidance I receive from my supervisor:

1	2	3	4	5	6	7

Very little.

Moderate.

Very much.

Figure 3-5 continued. Feedback Checklist.

1. In 1979 more systems people were excited because the profession was newer - the maturing of the profession.

2. In 1979 more people were doing development and now the shift is toward more dated legacy systems and technologies.

3. In 1979 the systems people were the experts on IT in the organization. As technology became more user friendly with the introduction of PCs and LANs, and more people coming into the organization had good computer skills, IT people lost some of their perceived status.

4. The large number of I/S graduates from business schools in the 1970s and 1980s did not find the job as exciting as the expectations set by business professors who were teaching information systems courses. These business graduates "spread the word" to future students and their brothers and sisters about this increasing job dissatisfaction. One outcome is that I/S college business majors has decreased dramatically in the 1980s. During this period, one I/S professional association actually made a video using CEOs from the major computer companies to tell high school students about the exciting career in computers. Although this effort was based upon good intentions, a better approach would have been to improve the meaningfulness of work within I/S departments rather than to further increase the expectations of future I/S majors in college.

5. And finally, once the excitement of having meaningful work (MPS) began to wear off in the 1980s, the movement from development to maintenance should have been accompanied with better management. If the job is providing less meaningfulness, then it is a good management practice to supplement that lack of job satisfaction with better goal setting, feedback, and career guidance. Information systems managers did not do this very well in the 1980s!

Conclusions and Recommendations for the 1990s:

1. Individual productivity leads to high job satisfaction. Give people meaningful work, set goals that are challenging but achievable in a reasonable time frame, give them a deadline, and then get out of their way. Remember, approximately 50-

60 percent of a software person's productivity is the match up of the job (MPS) and the person (GNS).

2. IT leaders should implement management strategies to increase the MPS of all jobs because of the tendency within the I/S profession to overhire people with superior technical skills and very high growth need strength. We recommend a brainstorming session of 10-15 systems people who do the same job. The objective of the session is to list ways to improve the job by improving the work process, increasing feedback or bureaucracy bashing (reverse engineering). Examples of bureaucracy bashing were presented in Chapter 2. After the brainstorming session, management should appoint a team to evaluate the suggestions and using the 80/20 rule, implement the two or three key changes that will have a major impact on the job's MPS. Then, give feedback to the team members on what ideas were implemented and what ideas were not implemented with the reasons for disapproval.

3. Improve feedback between managers and individual contributors. Poor feedback was a problem in 1979 and it still is a problem in 1995. One of the reasons for poor feedback is the low social need strength of systems people and the fact that there are few good role models within IT. We recommend that organizations require new project managers or coaches to attend a short course (using camcorders) on how to give and receive feedback. If a feedback course is not possible, the an alternative is to require that project managers and coaches use our *Feedback Checklist*.

4. Develop a strategy to change the mix of low SNS people. Consider training for your existing low SNS people, but also consider changing the selection process and sources of selecting new people to introduce more high SNS people as the IT organization moves from legacy systems to client-server. For example, we are aware of one East Coast financial institution that implemented a selection strategy of hiring liberal arts majors (higher SNS) for maintenance jobs, provided in-house COBOL training, and then placed them in "fixit" type maintenance jobs. The firm's findings were higher job satisfaction

and lower turnover with liberal arts graduates. Although we did not do the research, it would have been interesting also to track customer satisfaction with higher SNS people. We will discuss how to hire high SNS people in Chapter 6.

5. IT departments should set up assessment centers and select future leaders not only for their technical skills and high GNS, but for their communication and change skills. The key challenge for IT leaders in the 1990s is *how to implement effective change*.

6. IT leaders, in cooperation with the corporate human resources department, must create a true technical ladder. As we flatten organizations and move to self directed teams, there is less opportunity for advancement. Therefore, a technical career plan may begin with an entry level position such as associate member, to member, then specialist, to senior specialist, consultant, and finally senior consultant. Some firms making progress toward a true technical career path are 3M, AT&T and Xerox.[9]

7. As we move from hierarchical organizations to true learning organizations, IT leaders must examine, and hopefully implement, 360 degree goal setting and performance appraisals. One of the inputs into 360 degree goal setting and performance appraisal is the customer which will improve the partnership process. Further, IT leaders must have some part of the annual merit increase of the team members be based upon the input (ratings) of other team members. Those team based behaviors that are rewarded are repeated!

References

1. J. Daniel Cougar and Robert A. Zawacki, **Motivating and Managing Computer Personnel** (NY.: Wiley Interscience, 1980).

2. See Robert A. Zawacki, "Motivating IT People in the 90s: An "Alarming Drop" in Job Satisfaction," **The Software Practitioner**, November, 1993, pages 1-5 and Robert A. Zawacki, "Motivating the I/S People of the Future," **Information Systems Management**, Spring, 1992, pages 73-75.

3. This Chapter is a modification of Chapter 5 in D. D. Warrick and Robert A. Zawacki, **Supervisory Management** (NY.: Harper & Row, 1984) and Chapters 2 and 5 in J. D. Cougar and Robert A. Zawacki, op. cit.

4. See Leon Festinger, **A Theory of Cognitive Dissonance** (Stanford, CA.: Stanford University Press, 1957).

5. Frederick Herzberg, et. al., **The Motivation to Work**, 2d. ed.(NY.: Wiley, 1969). Also see Herzberg, "One More Time: How do You Motivate Employees," **Harvard Business Review**, September-October, 1987, pages 109-120.

6. For the complete background on core job theory, see A. N. Turner and P. R. Lawrence, **Industrial Jobs and the Worker** (Boston: Harvard Graduate School of Business Administration, 1965) and J. Richard Hackman and Greg R. Oldham, **Work Redesign** (Reading, MA.: Addison-Wesley, 1980).

7. The database is constantly changing and being updated. For example, we just completed an international study for the Help Desk Institute and determined norms for the jobs of call screening, 1st level support, 2nd level support, and help desk manager which was published in **Liferaft**, May, 1993, pages 1-14. We are currently investigating the MPS of people doing object oriented programming in the U.K. and the U.S.

8. Robert A. Zawacki, "How To Pick Eagles," **Datamation**, September 15, 1985, pages 115-116 and Robert A. Zawacki, "Abil-

ity, Motivation, and The Job Itself: What is the Relationship?" **Managing System Development**, June, 1993, pages 8-9.

9. Technical career paths were discussed at the **Seventh, Eighth, and Ninth Annual Symposiums for Human Resource Executives in Information Systems** during 1992, 1993, and 1994.

PART II

PEOPLE PROCESSES AND SYSTEMS TO SUPPORT THE TRANSFORMATION

Chapter 4

Examples, Issues, and Challenges of Teams in IT

Why Teams?

Anyone who doubts the strong effect of groups on individual behavior needs only to look at available research on group dynamics to conclude that individual behavior is highly influenced by co-workers in a team environment. The potential for a significant positive or negative effect on an individual's performance makes it imperative that IT managers understand group dynamics and, more importantly, learn how to develop high performance teams. How can an IT leader be more effective by using the knowledge of team dynamics?[1]

1. A knowledge of the key features of a high performance team can help an IT leader guide a team in designing appropriate norms and values, thus improving team behavior.

2. Knowing constructive and destructive behaviors in a team helps the IT manager facilitate the group in demonstrating healthy behaviors.

3. It can be used by the IT manager or the individuals in the team to continuosly improve group processes to create a learning team.

4. It can be used to design a team structure to facilitate goal accomplishment.

IT Team Processes

Most IT teams today have evolved into a more participative model where the work of the team belongs to the whole team and the team assigns tasks to the team members with the authority and skills needed to complete the tasks. Also, the team is a major part of the reward system and there is an open flow of information throughout the team. Organizational redesign *can not* take place without agreement from the team on the new processes. Planning for the team processes up front will save enormous amounts of time later on and reduce the potential for group conflict.

Teams are not created overnight. Rather, they are developed over time and are a journey without an end because of the need to create a learning team. Change is not revolutionary but evolutionary and a new team design that results in value added to the customer will not happen by proclamation. First, the IT manager needs to evaluate the IT team's current processes and envision what the new processes should be and how the team will get to this new design. What defines a team is that its members share the responsibility for achieving common goals, which is empowerment.

Team processes refer to the ways in which the team makes decisions, resolves conflict, interacts with one another and exerts influence or power. Team processes are the most important part of the team because they directly effect team performance. Progressive IT managers examine the teams processes with the individuals in the team to assure the processes are resulting in the desired performance levels.

Key Elements to Effective IT Teams

A high performance team practices continuous process improvement which results in high performance levels. The goal of an IT manager is to build the team process (norms, values and trust) which results in the following key elements.

1. Individuals have a good understanding and a commitment to the goals of the team.

2. Different individuals are utilized for different tasks, therefore the team maximizes its capabilities.

3. The team responds rapidly to change and opportunity.

4. Members feel a sense of responsibility for the team's performance.

5. Creativity, adaptability, and flexibility are rewarded.

6. The team continuously examines its processes and becomes a learning team.

7. The climate is trusting, non-intimidating and open.

8. Feedback is shared routinely and communication in all directions is encouraged.

Team Norms and Values

Team norms are defined as a standard shared by the individuals which regulate behavior within the team. Norms denote the processes by which groups regulate and set expectations about individuals' behavior in the team. Norms can develop very quickly, even in a team that is temporarily assigned for a particular application development project.

Team values are defined as the convictions or beliefs of the team. Values also have a direct effect on the teams performance. Typical IT values and norms are listed below in Figure 4-1.

Know who your customer is and take care of them. They are everything.

Trust and honesty are the cornerstones of our behavior within the team.

Our teamwork is based on the mutual respect we have for each other.

High quality IT applications is how we want to be known.

The honor of one is the honor of all.

We will make more correct decisions than bad. We value risk takers.

Our team will always strive to be a high performance team...

Figure 4-1. Example IT Team Values and Norms.

All IT teams should develop norms and values that will result in desired team outcomes. Norms and values can help the IT team survive when it is under threat from an external source. Norms and values provide a basis for goal-directed behavior when the team feels it needs to "circle the wagons". Further, it can also simplify expectations by letting each team member know what is expected of them. Finally, it can serve as a rallying point for all the individual group members.

Team Trust

The primary responsibility for creating a climate of openness and trust is with the IT manager or coach. The team usually looks to the IT manager to see if his actions and words are consistent. The manager typically has greater access to key information and can set the tone for interpersonal meetings. If an IT manager is intimidating or threatening in his actions this will only encourage the team to come together collectively to resist the change program. An IT manager can develop trust by encouraging openness and honesty.

Empowered individuals on a team are involved in key decisions, not excluded or indicted to from the top down. The team's performance is *not* characterized by lengthy bouts of discussion, which can only be described as the presentation and defense of different views, in search of the *best* view. Effective communications are more typically characterized by extensive dialogue, the free and creative exploration of complex and subtle issues through deep and attentive listening and the suspension of individual views, after a thorough discussion, for the benefit of the team. A trusted IT manager is one who can change direction if the information shown substantiates the change or can be influenced by the team's beliefs.

A team whose members trust each other typically will not take advantage of other team member's weaknesses. Tom Peters once said: " To move fast requires trust - period. Trust, though essentially interpersonal or one-on-one, is exhibited on a day-to-day basis by not signing up for what you can't deliver on."[2] Although trust is developed through a straightforward, fair, and honest process between individual team members, it can grow at a painfully slow rate. Sometimes it seems too slow a process. To build trust with team members, IT managers need to concentrate on six areas: communication, support, respect, fairness, predictability, and competence.[3]

1. **Communication** - is a matter of keeping subordinates informed, providing accurate feedback, explaining decisions and policies, being candid about one's own problems, and resisting the temptation to hoard information for use as a tool or a reward.

2. **Support** - showing concern for team members as people. It means being available and approachable. It means helping people, coaching them, encouraging their ideas, and defending their positions.

3. **Respect** - feeds on itself. The most important form of respect is delegation, and the second most important is listening to the team members and acting on their opinions.

4. **Fairness** - means giving credit where it is due, being objective and impartial in performance appraisals, and giving praise liberally. The opposite type of behavior is favoritism, hypocrisy, misappropriating ideas and accomplishments. Unethical behavior is difficult for a team member to forgive and highly destructive of trust. We observed an IT manager in a large defense contracting firm who claimed they had self directed teams; when we interviewed the team members, all told us that the team manager always took credit for their ideas. Thus, in this team, trust was very low and the team members were always suspicious of the leader's directives. It was ironic that the team leader actually believed he had trust with the team!

5. **Predictability** - is a matter of behaving consistently and dependably and of keeping both explicit and implicit promises. A broken promise can do considerable damage. If the team leader must break a promise, the team leader should "tell it like it is" as soon as possible and the team will take the broken promise as a temporary set back but then will move forward.

6. **Competence** - demonstrating technical and professional ability and good business sense. Employees don't want to be managed by a leader they see as incompetent. Trust grows from seeds of decent behaviors, but thrives on the admiration and respect that only a capable leader can command.

If an IT manager concentrates on and practices these six areas, then the elusive benefit of trust will develop. Organizations and individuals build "trust accounts' that operate similar to bank accounts. Individuals will make "mental" deposits and build their own trust reserve by concentrating on the above areas. IT managers can make mistakes resulting in a withdrawal from this reserve. The wise IT manager always makes sure the reserve is in the black and not in the red. Once the reserve is in the red, the manager becomes less effective, will be increasingly scrutinized and flexibility disappears.

Stages in Team Development

Research indicates another factor influencing the teams effectiveness is the development of the team. Several research based theories suggest most teams progress through five stages. These 5 stages are referred to by the deceptively simple titles *forming, storming, norming, performing*, and *adjourning*.[4] In our STAR organization we refer to these five stages as: one-on-one supervision, group manager, team coordinator, boundary leader interface, and resource staff.

1. *Forming* - In the first stage of development, when group members first come together, emphasis is usually placed on making acquaintances, sharing information, testing each other, and so forth. Group members attempt to discover which interpersonal behaviors are acceptable or unacceptable in the team. In this stage they depend upon other team members for providing cues to acceptable behavior.

2. *Storming* - In the second stage of group development, a high degree of intergroup conflict (storming) can usually be expected as group members attempt to develop a place for themselves and to influence the development of group norms and roles. Issues are discussed more openly, and efforts are made to clarify group goals.

3. *Norming* - Over time, the group begins to develop a sense of oneness. Here, group norms emerge (norming) to guide each individual's behavior. Group members come to accept other team members and develop a unity of purpose that binds them together.

4. *Performing* - Once group members agree on their basic purpose, they set about developing separate roles for the various members. In this final stage, role differentiation emerges to take advantage of task specialization in order to facilitate the goal attainment of the team.

5. *Adjourning* - Is the process of grieving the loss of a team member or the disbanding of a work team. In today's environment of downsizing, it is imperative that IT managers allow for the recognition of this stage. This stage is also known as the separation stage. In the STAR (learning) organization, this stage is especially important because of the use of temporary teams, such as, rapid application development teams.

As the IT team matures, the managers need to recognize the differing stages of development and always help to push the team toward the *performing* stage. Although the model is simplistic in design, not all stages are proceeded through sequentially; rather it provides a generalized conceptual scheme concerning development over time. Once again, teams are evolutionary not revolutionary. In a learning organization, teams learn from their achievements and mistakes, and they build in team meetings to reflect and gain insight. Then, they disseminate that new insight to all team members and other teams.

Cutting Edge Types of Teams in IT

Self Directed Teams. Ask IT managers whether they believe their organizations can have employee to manager span of control ratios 40 to 1, and chances are they'll say you cannot do this and maintain customer service; however, many IT organization are doing just that and more! Quality, adding value to the bottom line, and customer satisfaction did not suffer, while productivity increased! But it does require a paradigm switch that encourages team members taking risks, empowering them, and an organizational design that puts this philosophy into practice.

IT organizations in certain Fortune 500 companies have already implemented self-directed teams, based on a participative management approach, that gives IT individuals the skills to handle change and make better business and technical decisions. Because they broaden their expertise, these IT individuals become more productive, motivated and satisfied with their jobs. For example, a systems analyst who has been trained in conflict resolution or interview skills would have not only the technical expertise to deliver the application design but also the managerial skills to make the implementation successful to the customer.[5]

In a traditional hierarchical IS department, managers are managers. They set goals and deadlines and generally control the situation. In a self-directed team (SDT), the leader's role evolves into one of counselor and consultant to the group. See Figure 4-2 below for a description of the journey from a top down control model to a Stage 5 empowered team.[6]

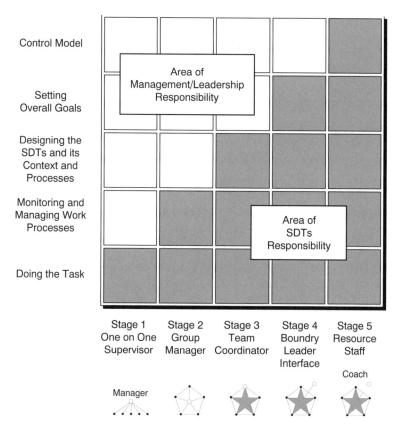

Figure 4-2. From Management Control to Self Control.

Our research indicates that about 50 percent of top-down control managers can make the transition to coach. Further, managers who have a healthy self-concept and are flexible, and are egoless can make this transition faster. Confident managers are the ones who get their feelings of self worth, not only from getting IT projects out the door, but also from watching people develop into well- rounded individuals. They are better prepared to hand control of the job to team members.

An example of an IT organization that transitioned from a control model to a coaching model is Digital Equipment Corporation. The giant Boston computer company decided to empower its people through a partnership approach in their Customer Support Centers. The partnership approach changed how the employees thought about their jobs. The coaches and team members were involved from the beginning of the redesign until the group reached the level of a complete self-directed team. Careful planning needs to take place to insure the design and implementation time frame is appropriate. Figure 4-3 illustrates a typical time reference.

As the team matures, becomes more responsible and develops the skills and competencies, many of the activities in Figure 4-3 are transferred to it. Some activities or tasks may be retained by the coach and that is fine. The key to developing and keeping trust is when the coach - up front - tells the team the activities he wishes to keep. For example, at one division the IT manager said he did not want to give up the budget. Great! Tell the team members up front and set realistic expectations. In another organization, the president said, "In our organization, individual contributors do not select their boss!" This is all right, but the coach must set realistic expectations and tell the team that they will never select their coach which is normally the situation in Stage 5.

After technical training, the team members need extensive training in the "people skills". Our research finds that training costs increase fourfold and most of that money is used in the "soft areas". Proper training is a must - up front. Do not start the SDT without some training on how problems will be resolved. Recently we encountered an IT organization that tried to push the group norming process, thinking they could fit in the training later. Six months into the teaming process, the Director of MIS called us and said "If only I had listened to you and done the training

Activity	Design and Implementation Time Reference						
	Before	3 months	6 months	12 months	18 months	24 months	30 months
1. Steering Committee	▓	▓	▓	▓	▓	▓	▓
2. Leadership/Coach Responsibilities	▓						
3. Team Member Responsibilities	▓						
4. Goals	▓						
5. Assumptions							
a. About SDTs	▓						
b. About People							
6. Training							
a. Technical & Quality		▓					
b. People Skills							
Problem Solving		▓					
Team Building			▓	▓	▓	▓	
Conducting Meetings			▓				
Presentation Skills				▓			
Conflict Resolution					▓		
Change Skills					▓		▓
c. Management Skills							
Interviewing					▓		
Feedback & Coaching					▓		
Performance Appraisal						▓	
Group Rewards		▓			▓		
Budgets							▓
7. Measurement							
a. Internal		▓	▓				
b. Customer Service					▓	▓	
8. Feedback							
a. Team		▓	▓	▓	▓	▓	
b. Other SDTs		▓	▓	▓	▓	▓	▓

Figure 4-3. Checklist for Self Directed Teams.

first! Now we have conflict within the team and are swimming up stream."

After developing its problem-solving skills, the team needs early training in team-building skills which focus on process (relationship) behavior. We recommend that while a team is in Stages 1 & 2, members begin to rate each other on group behavior at least every 2 weeks. These ratings should be reviewed at a Monday morning team meeting. Self evaluations can be done every three weeks during Stage 3 and once a month in Stages 4 & 5. Team evaluations and feedback permit the team to learn, adjust, and grow. The Commercial Aircraft Division of Hamilton Standard learned that team-building is a continuous process and teams need a "buck-up" session about every six months.

Rules for Implementing SDTs.

1. Set up a steering committee with top-management support and plan a long range effort with a pilot SDT. Further, select a natural work group committed to employee empowerment and who are involved in a technology/product/service with task interdependencies. The pilot SDT should have a manager with a high probability of succeeding as a coach. SDTs are more successful when the team has a solid foundation of technical skills, but also have excellent people skills.

2. Establishing base line measures of internal team satisfaction and external customer service.

3. Visiting other IT organizations with SDTs to determine "best practices".

4. Making certain that the pilot SDT is congruent with organizational values and goals. Recognize that designing and implementing SDTs is a cultural shift for the organization.

Some of the values for the implementation of SDTs are:

*   People will set goals and strive to meet those goals.

*   People who are committed and care about their work will improve upon new methods of doing work.

*   People enjoy growing and want meaningful work.

• People seek many satisfactions in work like: pride in achievement, sense of contribution and new challenges.

5. Think beyond cutting costs. There usually is an actual drop in productivity during the early stages of a SDT, because the team members are learning new skills, conducting team meetings, and are more involved in the planning process. Be patient - as the team grows and the individuals members feel they are truly empowered, the gains are greater productivity, lower costs, higher quality products, greater customer service, and more adaptability. It may be 18 to 24 months before the organization begins to see the positive results of the change program.

6. Recognize that many managers are threatened by even the mention of SDTs. No longer the experts, now managers must become coaches or facilitators. As we indicated above, it is our experience that only about one-half of existing managers can make the transition, even after training in the new competencies. Organization leaders must clearly state expectations up front: that good performers who cannot make the transition to coaches will be retained as individual contributors as long as they add value to the bottom line.

7. The performance appraisal and compensation systems must be congruent with the concept of SDTs. Consider greater employee participation into reward decisions and designing gainsharing plans and profit-sharing schemes that encourage horizontal organizational structures based on process, rather than function. At about the 18-month point, consider changing the reward from individual to part group/individual. Consider a bonus for the volunteers in the first pilot SDT.

8. Establish feedback systems to inform all members of the organization on the progress of the pilot and future SDTs. Consider having SDT members brief top leaders on their progress. Feedback permits the program to adjust, grow and remain viable over time. Successful SDTs are in a constant state of self-learning and self-correcting.

9. Consider starting other SDTs soon after the pilot SDT has

Instructions: Answer each question true or false. Then go to the answers to determine your score.

1. Because the SDT discusses and approves all issues, the decision-making process of a SDT is time consuming and inefficient.

2. Members on the SDT are seen as equal contributors to the business thus it is a leaderless organization.

3. Since there are little to no rules or structure in a SDT, everyone does what he or she wants to do all day.

4. Designing a SDT takes many hours of planning, training, and coaching to be successful.

5. Peer appraisals are an effective way of managing performance in a SDT and should be one of the first design areas to be implemented.

6. Being a coach of a SDT is easier than a traditional team. The coach has little to do since the members are now doing all the work.

7. It is difficult to change an existing organization into a SDT if the individual team members are not technically and managerially competent.

8. Decisions are supported and effective when made by individuals in teams who are directly doing the job and are impacted the most by the decision.

9. All current managers can transition into a coaching role.

10. Members of a SDT can hire their own manager/coach.

Figure 4-4. A Quiz on Self Directed Teams.

demonstrated success. An excellent time to start new SDTs is immediately after the pilot team receives a bonus.

10. Finally, team members need a *vision* from the IT leadership team combined with *trust, resources* and *time* to implement the new structure.

More and more companies are moving toward SDTs. It is one way organizations in the 1990s are strategically redesigning the workplace to produce a high performance organization that has a competitive advantage. But there are many people within these organizations who have not made the paradigm shift from a traditional and bureaucratic management structure to a learning organization based on autonomous work teams. There are many misunderstandings concerning this new organizational strategy and structure. Your beliefs about SDTs could be undermining your organization's success at effectively implementing this change. To test your knowledge of the fact and fiction of SDTs, answer the questions (Figure 4-4) true or false.

Answers to the SDT Quiz:
Give yourself one point for each correct answer.

1. False - In a SDT, all decisions are not discussed and approved by the team. It is important that before evolving to a SDT the decision making process is developed and accepted by the team. In some cases, individual team members are empowered to make commitments for the entire team. If the commitment of the team is needed for a particular issue, then individuals on the team should get together to share ideas and suggestions. But, the final decision might rest with the coach, it may reflect the input of the individuals or it may be true team participation, in more of a democratic sense. Where the decision-making authority lies with different types of decisions needs to be discussed with the team, otherwise, team members will not understand what authority they have when trying to make group decisions. Decisions requiring the approval of the team will take longer to come to consensus but research indicates that implementation time will be shorter and the commitment will be greater.

2. False - All members are not equal contributors but are acknowledged as having different and valued skills that help the team achieve their goals. Members responsibilities include scheduling, training, performance appraisals, recognition, rewards, promotions, vacations or leaves of absence to the team. The individuals of the team will shift work priorities and assignments to meet the ever changing business demands. The

team will assign work to members based on individual development needs thus causing the team to be highly flexible and multiskilled. Finally, the leadership on the team is rotated between team members, once again, based on the individual development needs. Individuals don't control the position but serve as a facilitator and coordinator within the different leadership roles. Thus, an SDT is not a leaderless organization but an organization with multiple leaders representing the team on multiple issues.

3. False - Structure is present in a SDT, otherwise, this type of approach will be nothing less than redesigned chaos. Boundaries, rules and structure are defined by the group via vision, values, norms, responsibilities and assumptions. These assumptions might be very different than a traditionally managed team that is more control oriented. Examples of the assumptions of a SDT include: individuals are valued, the team is seen as the means for getting work done, the individuals doing the job can make the best decisions about the business. The boundaries define the SDT context in which individuals perform. The team values honesty, attacking problems not people, assertiveness with caring, active listening, calmness, patience, self-control, assuming the best about people, achieving team goals rather than individual goals, and exceeding the business needs. Structure and rules are adapted and evaluated on a business needed basis and are usually highly flexible to reach the team goals.

4. True - Vision, values, norms, assumptions, and responsibilities need to be defined and accepted by all team members and the coach before implementing a SDT. This can take a lot of time and planning but if this pre-work is not done, much energy will be spent down the road because team members are not aligned with the SDT philosophy and goals. By setting the stage for alignment with the SDT approach the team understands and buys into all expectations.

5. False - Peer appraisals are rarely used in traditional work groups but are used quite often in SDTs. Peers are often in a better position to observe their co-workers for a longer period

of time and in a broader variety of situations than a traditional manager. As a result of this close contact, peers have a greater opportunity to provide accurate feedback. But a common design failure of some organizations is to implement peer appraisal immediately after evolving from a traditional team to a SDT. Peer appraisals can only be successful after the team has matured, where there are good communication skills, feedback skills, and trust between members. Conflict resolution is an art and not all members of the team will want to evaluate a peer's performance until they feel there is mutual respect and trust of their peers. Some SDTs are evaluated by their customers. This process combined with peer evaluations is known as 360 degree performance appraisal.

6. False - Being a coach of a SDT is not easier than being a traditional manager. A coach is more of a team resource and acts as a consultant to the team. Since the team is fully responsible and accountable for their outputs, the coach no longer has position power, but more often has the power to only influence. The coach's role change and the new competencies consist of long term strategic planning, representing the team to top management in getting a team budget, mentoring new employees in the SDT paradigm, guiding the team in setting performance goals, communication skills in all directions (presenting the team's issues to top management), and overseeing the evolution of the SDT development process.

7. True - A newly formed group may need some additional training in skills to make the team successful. An assessment of each team member may find a lack in skills such as conflict resolution, interviewing skills, budget negotiation, time management, collaborative politics, interpersonal skills, problem solving, listening, facilitation, and feedback. Without the proper training, team members may feel overwhelmed by the new responsibilities and tasks. Decisions may be adversely effected because of lack of these skills. The commitment to multiskilled team members is not without cost, both in time and money, but it is viewed as an investment. As a result of training, team members have an unusually broad set of busi-

ness and technical skills. Adaptability to change and productivity is very high because of the multiskilled team.

8. True - The style of SDTs assumes that individual members of the team will take part personally in the decision-making process and will be more likely to have an increased commitment to the objectives and goals of the team and the company. Also, by having the team make more decisions about the day to day business, the decisions are usually better. The whole is greater than the sum of the parts. Even if the leader of the project knows much more than anyone else, the unique knowledge of other individuals on the team could be the source of gaps in knowledge of the leader. Therefore, individuals doing the job should be involved in making decisions because of their collective wisdom and commitment.

9. False - All managers will not want to or be capable of transitioning into a coaching role. In a traditional management role, the supervisor is responsible for the total outputs and commitments of the group. The traditional supervisor is more control-oriented and is usually chosen because he was the most technically qualified in the group. After the transition to a SDT, members will need less control and will work independently. The traditional supervisor might not want to work in a coaching role where the team is in control. The team will be responsible for training, peer appraisals, rewards, promotions, vacations, scheduling and budget allocation. Some traditional managers might not have the ability or people skills to work in a SDT. The traditional manager might not want to work in an environment of less control or may be incapable of sharing power.

10. True - Team members can and have hired their own coach. Before starting the process, pre-work should be done to load the process for success. Core competencies of a coach are different than a traditional manager. Once the team has agreed on the core competencies and the hiring action committee is formed, then the candidates are pre-screened over the phone. Interviewers should listen for a coach's previous work that is conducive to team involvement. Words like "we" and "they"

would be more appropriate than a candidate who only talks about "my workers" or "I". During the interviews, scenarios can be used to determine team interaction skills and the understanding of the SDT philosophy.

Scoring the Quiz:

8-10 points - Your knowledge of self-directed teams is high and your beliefs about a SDT are very accurate. You have a good understanding of the differences between a traditionally managed team and a SDT.

5-7 points - Your knowledge of SDTs is equal to that of most people. Further discovery of the dynamics of SDTs could be beneficial to your career.

4-0 points - Your knowledge of SDTs is low. You should consider additional development and investigation of the SDT philosophy before trying to implement or work on designing a SDT.

Virtual Teams at Telephone Express. New technologies such as electronic mail, personal computers and the fax machine facilitated the introduction of another form of teams which are called virtual teams. Designing and implementing a virtual team requires all of the processes and skills detailed above. However, it also requires additional skills because the team members are normally located at great distances from each other and yet they must perform as a team. Rather than describe virtual teams from a theoretical perspective, we believe it will be more meaningful to present an actual case study.

Case Study. Telephone Express, located in Colorado Springs, is on the fast-track to becoming a national leader of high-performance telecommunication and information age services. In 1992, its first year of eligibility, Telephone Express made the prestigious **Inc. Magazine** list of the 500 fastest growing privately held U.S. companies. It ranked first in Colorado and 13th in the nation. Telephone Express is one of the largest long distance carriers based in the Rocky Mountain region with 1994 sales of more than $42 million and 250 employees in six states.

In 1987, John Street and Mary Beazley founded TeleConcepts, Inc. as a vehicle for acquiring the assets of a financially troubled long distance carrier - Telephone Express. Both owners became involved in the telecommunications industry in 1986 while consulting for a small, struggling long distance company. As experienced CPAs, their keen attention to detail helped them realize the company's problems were due largely to mistakes in customer billing, poor network administration, ineffective financial planning, and a lack of focused customer service. Street and Beazley also suspected the high failure rate among other long distance companies was related to these problems. By taking smaller, faltering companies and combining them into one efficient operation, Street and Beazley believed that they could offer customers improved quality, services, and support. By 1991 Telephone Express had surpassed $18 million in annual sales. But, this was just the beginning. Sales approached the $22 million mark in 1992, and the company boasted revenues of $31 million in 1993.

The young company, however, made sure its growth didn't lead to the carelessness that had sunk its predecessors. While introducing better service and products to its newly acquired customers, Telephone Express also developed a strong customer service plan. A large piece of this high quality customer service philosophy is being delivered through the pro-active Major Accounts Department.

In the Major Accounts Department a new form of team redesign is taking shape where employees work remotely and are located across a six state region. The work is performed in the local office, at home or in a hotel and is transmitted electronically to the corporate headquarters. This virtual team takes advantage of several of the latest electronic media, including personal computers, fax machines, cellular phones, E-mail, and other communication via the Internet. At Telephone Express the advantage of virtual teams is that the individual contributors stay closer to the customer and can still receive and transmit information, using modems attached to their computers, back to the corporate office. This pro-active customer service is available 24 hours a day and these empowered and knowledgeable troubleshooters have the experience to solve their customer's problems. When a hard copy is required, a fax machine can be employed.

Just how does this "virtual team" stay in contact with each other and their coach? In most cases, the team comes together quarterly to review and establish new goals. Team members also use the quarterly meetings for training and continuous improvement sharing with their peers. A weekly conference call via the telephone is used to keep the remote members informed of updated new procedures, issues or regulatory changes.

Profile of a Good Virtual Team Member. What are the competencies of the individuals who work successfully in virtual teams?

1. Internally motivated - Since the work is usually performed independently, the individual needs to be a self-starter. Goals or measurements should not focus on hours worked but should be results oriented. Examples include customer cancellation percentage, completion of projects on time or zero defects.

2. Competent - It is much more difficult to handle a performance issue when the employee is remote. Therefore, it is imperative that clear goals are established and understood by all team members. The employee should have all the training and skills necessary to perform the job at a minimal level before starting to work remotely.

3. Self-starter - Since the manager is not physically in contact daily and only truly sets goals quarterly, the individual needs to understand his or her job. The individual should not need a lot of direction from the coach. Individuals in this situation are usually people perceived to be low maintenance employees.

4. Independent worker - The employee might not be in contact with anyone from the home office or team for months, therefore they need to be self sufficient and do not necessarily need a lot of socialization from peers at work.

5. Resourceful - Obviously, there should be available the resources necessary to accomplish performance levels, but what happens if the computer link is down to the home office or the manager is unavailable to discuss an issue? The individual needs to be able to handle these stressful situations and still work toward furthering the goals.

Challenges for the Team. Some of the challenges facing a virtual team are:

1. Keeping communication channels open. Since the individuals in the virtual team are located remotely, a feeling of isolation can occur. Changes in policy and procedures need to be relayed as soon as possible to the individuals on the team. The IT manager must keep in contact as much as possible utilizing technology (Internet, E-mail, fax, U.S. mail or telephone). Additionally, the managers/coaches need to be as assessable as possible to the employees who are working remotely. It is difficult enough that they are out of sight but you do not want them to get the misleading impression that they are also out of mind.

2. Cohesiveness of the team. The IT manager should monitor and effect cohesiveness by getting agreement on goals/direction of the team, enhance interactions within the team, and focus on the competition.

This type of team is especially conducive to the knowledge worker of this decade. Additionally, as more families have two or more employed workers, as highway traffic increases in our major cities, more and more knowledge workers will be working from their home or remote locations. Some virtual teams will have all team members working remotely or just a handful may be located away from the team. With the growing global labor pool, this new design will become more and more common place. Some software companies are already permitting their people to work on projects at remote locations. We are aware of one West Coast software organization that permitted a high performing systems programmer to relocate to a farm in Iowa and still remain on the development team.

Tiger Teams at Wheels Inc. Larry Runge of Wheels Incorporated recommends a three pronged approach to building client-server development teams which he calls "Tiger Teams."[7] As the old organization moves toward the learning organization (STAR), and the corresponding movement from legacy systems to client-server, it is easy for the development people to become overwhelmed with the change program, unless three straightforward guidelines are followed:

1. "Hire as many people as your budget will allow who already have the skills you need."

2. "Immediately bring in contract personnel with the requisite skills and experience to get things rolling."

3. "Begin aggressive training of your internal staff."[7]

Conclusions and Recommendations for the 1990s

1. In this chapter we discussed the reasons for using teams to develop systems, the key elements of effective teams, and the stages of team growth and development. We believe teams will be one of the key building blocks of the organization of the future.

2. Because of the low social need strength (SNS) of systems people, implementing teams will be a difficult but not an impossible process.

3. Leaders of the future should be selected, not only for their technical skills, but for their ability to coach teams.

4. Some of the major types of teams are: self directed teams (SDTs), virtual teams, and tiger teams.

5. For teams to be successful in IT and to move the people involved from single-loop learning to double-loop learning, human resource systems must be implemented that reinforce team values and behavior. Some examples of progressive human resource systems are: assessment centers, individual contributors evaluating and selecting new team members, 360 degree performance appraisal, a true technical career track, and a competency based pay system.

References

1. D. D. Warrick and Robert A. Zawacki, **High Performance Management** (N.Y.: Harper and Row Publishers, 1984), page 160.

2. Tom Peters, **Thriving on Chaos** (N.Y.: Knopf, 1987), page 514.

3. This is a modification from Fernando Bartolome, "Nobody Trusts the Boss Completely - Now What?" **Harvard Business Review,** 67 (Mar-Apr,1989), pages 137-139.

4. B. Tuckman and M. Jensen, "Stages of Small Group Development Revisited," **Group and Organizational Studies,** 1977, pp. 419-442.

5. Carol A. Norman and Robert A. Zawacki, "Breaking Appraisal Tradition," **Computerworld,** April 1, 1991, page 78 and Robert A. Zawacki, "Do I/S and Teams Mix?" **Computerworld,** June 13, 1994, page 122.

6. Robert A. Zawacki and Carol A. Norman, "Self-Directed Teams in IT: Friend or Foe?" **Labnotes,** Vol. 2:1., 1993, pages 4-6.

7. Larry Runge, "Tiger Teams," **CIO,** February 1, 1995, pages 22-24.

Chapter 5
Goals and Performance Appraisal Systems to Support the STAR Organization

Searching for the Holy Grail

Ever since the beginning of organizations, leaders have been searching for the holy grail in a performance appraisal system. As we move from individual to team performance in information technology organizations, that search is taking on a new emphasis.

From the beginning of Adam Smith's task specialization theories and the administrative bureaucracy of Max Weber until the 1960s the major type of performance appraisal system used by most organizations was the traditional system, which had forms such as the graphic rating scale or the forced distribution scale. This was a top down system that had a heavy evaluative and judgmental tone. In the early 1960s, many IT leaders began to realize the traditional performance appraisal system only emphasized *how managers rated people* and did not look at *what happened to people when they were rated.*

Thus, in the 1960s, performance appraisal moved from judgmental systems to developmental systems and the new approach became management by objectives and behavioral anchored rating scales. This progressive group of IT leaders were interested not only in rating people, but also in *what happens to individual contributors' attitudes and behaviors* when they are given feedback on their performance.

In the 1990s, as IT organizations moved into the decade of superior customer service, value added to the customer, time-based competition, and team-based management, the need for multiple inputs into the performance appraisal process has taken on new meaning. Out of a need to reinforce these movements, 360 degree goal setting and performance appraisal emerged.

360 Degree Goal Setting. The 360 degree goal setting process differs from the traditional supervisor-subordinate goal setting meeting because this new method involves a diverse sampling of internal and external customers. In addition to supervisor-subordinate goal setting, this 360 degree process of goal setting creates a mutual agreement between a supplier and customer on their relationship and expectations of each other. Figure 5-3 indicates the relationship between 360 degree goal setting, 360 degree performance appraisal and rewards. Early experiences by firms such as Federal Express, Hamilton Standard, and Digital indicate the following advantages:

1. Greater two-way communication between the organization and external customers.

2. More commitment and accountability to external customers.

3. Increased role clarification.

4. Promotes employee development and teamwork.

5. Improved reliability and validity of the goal setting process.

360 Degree Performance Appraisal. Typically, once a year performance appraisals are unproductive, but they don't have to be. Some teams have changed to a more participatory performance appraisal system which has inputs from all directions - 360 degree performance appraisal. This approach has radically changed the way employees value and think about their jobs. Because team members can and should be involved in the decisions that effect their day-to-day business lives, this new human resource system is receiving a very positive response from individual contributors and coaches. Similarly, individuals should be involved in evaluating other team members' performance via a 360 degree appraisal process. In more traditional organizations, these decisions are made only by the manager. In a more autonomous team the coach is involved with team members on a business level. Further, the coach facilitates the team's direction and coordinates or interfaces with other managers in traditionally managed work groups.

How Does 360 Degree Work?

Multiple individuals from various sources in the organization and external customers fill out a performance appraisal document on each team member. Questions are answered concerning everything from how articulate that team member is, to their trustworthiness. Also, the person being rated (ratee) completes a performance appraisal form on themselves. The inputs from all sources are gathered by the coach or in some teams a peer is used, who is labeled an advocate. The ratee then gets to compare their opinion of themselves to those of the group who participated: peers, external customers, suppliers and the coach or manager. Some organizations which currently are using such a system include Ford Microelectronics, Digital Equipment Corporation, Johnson & Johnson Advanced Behavioral Technology, AT&T, Federal Express, and Pitney Bowes. Interestingly, only about a third of managers produce assessments that match what the ratee's peers see in their co-worker.[1] Also, the above process has been used in many of the above organizations to understand better the effectiveness of a manager or team coordinator. It has been used by subordinates to evaluate their manager.

Figure 5-1. Performance Management System.

In a traditional appraisal process, the manager typically is the sole input for the appraisal and managers realize there is no way for them to know whether an employee is an effective performer in all interactions, or whether the employee is only an effective performer when the manager is around.

What can a manager do when an employee is perceived as effective by the manager but the co-workers or customers do not have the same perception? Truly, can a manager evaluate an employee that they only see a few short hours a day? Therefore, there is a true need for an accurate, subjective and fair performance instrument. The answer may lie in the 360 degree performance appraisal system, not only for the employee, but at all levels of the learning organization. What makes up the foundation of a 360 degree system?

The Foundation of the Process. To ensure that measuring the employee's performance is rooted in job content, the performance appraisal committee or coach should develop an accurate and extensive document outlining the job requirements. These requirements are used to identify the critical activities that demonstrate job success and the tasks against which the employee is measured. This document is crucial, because it sets the team's expectations for individual behavior. Once the document is developed, the team should review it and if no further changes are warranted, accept the requirements.

After documenting and communicating the job requirements, the following steps are followed to ensure valid and meaningful appraisals of each individual on a team. First, the person to be evaluated is notified by electronic mail that her performance appraisal is due. Then, the secretary sends a notice by electronic mail to the person 30 days before the scheduled time. Next the person being rated (ratee) chooses an advocate or committee chair who is usually a peer within the team. The advocate or committee chair selects the other members of the committee. Typically, there are four committee members: the ratee, the chairperson, the coach, and another team member.

As soon as possible, the ratee sends e-mail to the team members, including the coach, outlining his or her accomplishments and training for the past year. This information is used as a basis for their input. An issue to resolve, before implementing 360 degree performance appraisal, is how many team members should rate the person and who should do the rating. As a rule of thumb, companies generally select between five and ten raters. Typically, less than five raters will limit the perspective on the employee's performance over the year. Over ten raters, is too complex and time-consuming.[2] Potential raters should have extensive interaction with the ratee.

The input from the team members and the customer is then

collected by the chairperson (advocate) and a copy of all of the inputs is sent to the individual being evaluated.

Internal Pool	External Pool
Manager/Coach Middle and Top Management Subordinates Peers/Team members Other Department Representatives	Suppliers Clients/Customers

Figure 5-2. Potential Pool for Feedback from Customers

Next, the individual contributor completes his or her own performance appraisal from the input received by the advocate. Then, the individual contributor sends a copy of the self appraisal document to the committee for its review. The document and all inputs are reviewed, which takes about a week, and the committee and the ratee meet for a detailed discussion of performance for the past year. If the performance document needs further revision or additional input, another meeting is scheduled. If not, a final rating is determined based on the input, and the committee uses 360 degree goal setting to establish goals for the next year. Also, this committee is responsible for providing guidance and counseling on the development plan of the ratee.

Finally, the advocate writes a summary of the meeting, including the rating and any promotion (if applicable). The completed performance appraisal is typed and signed by the members of the committee, ratee and the coach. It is then submitted to the personnel department for review and filing.

As a performance appraisal system, the 360 degree approach can be time-consuming, and the gains don't come easily, but the rewards are an increase in employee commitment and productivity. Remember, an effective decision is equal to the right decision times the commitment to the decision. When individuals don't have any voice in how or when they do their jobs, goals established from above may have little or no meaning. When employees have a voice in negotiating their performance goals, they have more commitment and the team members are then empowered to accomplish the goals.

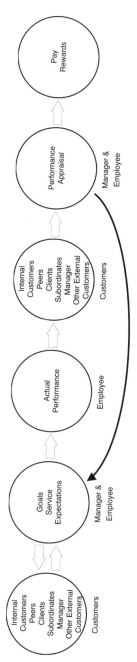

Figure 5-3. 360 Degree Goal Setting and Performance Appraisal Process.

Advantages and Disadvantages of the Process

Advantages. The process has many advantages.[3] Some of those advantages are:

1. The team member receives feedback from the people (peers and the customer) who are the most familiar with his or her daily performance. Because these individuals are very close to the team member, observations of performance are normally more accurate than those individuals who do not observe the performance on a daily basis.

2. Many self directed teams have a ratio of one coach to forty team members. Because performance appraisal input is provided by different sources, the manager has more time to mentor team members and provide for the future direction and strategy of the team. Also, the team coach does not have to be both judge and counselor. The coach can listen to team inputs and at the same time share responsibilities for the individual's appraisal with the rest of the committee.

3. The responsibility to get the appraisal done is on the individual's shoulders; therefore, they are seldom late! Motivated employees seek out the information as a form of accurate feedback. Individuals like to know their team is aware of what they are doing and they like to be recognized for their contributions.

4. Feedback of acceptable and unacceptable behavior is given in a more timely manner. Research indicates that feedback is most effective when it closely follows the behavior to which it relates.

5. The individual is involved in the goal setting process. This allows for individual goals to be integrated with team, customer and organizational goals. Employees who feel empowered to effect change see themselves in control of their jobs and career.

6. Team members are groomed for leadership roles in other teams because they understand and have participated in the perfor-

mance appraisal process, interviews, scheduling and decisions on the direction of the business.

7. A major benefit of 360 degree performance appraisal is increased accountability of employees to their customers.

    Disadvantages. Many of the advantages are offset by disadvantages. Some of those are:[3]

1. The process can be time consuming. Five to ten individuals need to provide input into the 360 degree performance appraisal. Additionally, finding time from a customer can be an additional problem. Although external customers feedback is critical to the process, don't survey external customers excessively. The customer may feel uncomfortable with the idea, particularly if it is a new situation. Make sure the process is mutually beneficial.

2. People may feel uncomfortable writing their own performance appraisals. They may feel as if they are "tooting their own horns," instead of summarizing what the teams input reflects. Also, they may need extensive training on how to write a good performance appraisal.

3. Team members may make errors in rating because of lack of education, experience or skills. The most common errors are:

    *   The *halo* effect - rating a team member high in one quality, which in turn effects the rating in another quality that does not deserve to be rated as high.

    *   *Strict* rating - consistently rating other team members lower than the normal or average, or being too harsh.

    *   *Lenient* rating - consistently rating other team members higher than the average (such rating errors can be seen in any performance system, but this occurs more often if the team members have not been trained.)

4. Fear of playing God - fear of the potentially adverse effects of providing input (It may not be easy to judge other team members.) It may not be easy for a customer to provide input; some customers have refused out of fear of legal action.

5. Competition for current and future rewards within the team can have an impact on the validity of the rating. The issue of whether the feedback from the various raters should be kept anonymous or be identified openly to the employee being reviewed must be resolved. Confidentiality can reduce the possibility that the employee will later confront the raters, and thus encourages raters to be more open and honest with their feedback. However, confidentiality has its own baggage because ratees often try to "hunt the ghost down" or figure out which rater provided the negative feedback.[2] Some groups have chosen to institute a rule that no rater can give negative feedback in the appraisal unless the rater has previously given the feedback directly to the ratee.

Considerations Before Implementing 360 Degree Performance Appraisal

Because of the radically different assumptions on which a 360 degree appraisal is based, there are many considerations that should be evaluated before adopting this type of system. Implementing an effective 360 degree appraisal process is not a knee-jerk reaction. Rather, this process requires significant up front work.

1. Training should be available for all raters because many might not have previously participated in appraisals. Lack of experience and skills can cause the process to become dysfunctional. The rater might become frustrated and stressed if the atmosphere is not collaborative. If proper training is not given, new team members may view the process as a threat. Training in conflict resolution, negotiation skills, legally defensible interviewing and interpersonal communications should also be considered.

2. The coach must continue to nurture, through communications, to ensure that the team is aligned with the 360 degree appraisal approach. Keeping communication channels open between team members is essential to ensure timely feedback. If channels break down, the process can become meaningless.

3. Individuals need to understand the process thoroughly and then

commit to it completely. Because some individuals may see this process as threatening, when interviewing potential organization members, extensive time should be spent on the organization's expectations concerning their participation in this type of approach to performance appraisal.

4. Inputs should be reviewed by the coach to prevent harsh and blatantly inaccurate statements. Also, a meeting with the people who provide inappropriate input might be necessary to guide them on appropriate content for input into the process. Input that is given directly to an individual, especially when the process is still new, may result simply in destructive feelings, which will need to be attended to later.

5. The process should be seen as collaborative. All key players are there to make the process easy, accurate, meaningful and helpful for the team.

Normally, the 360 degree performance appraisal process is not implemented with a team until the team has worked together for 12 to 18 months. In the early stages of team formation, our experience indicates other issues take priority and the team needs extensive training in the history of performance appraisal, how to give feedback, how to make decisions as a team, and the most important: getting the product out the door while transforming from a top down control model to a team environment.

A 360 degree performance appraisal system will be successful if these considerations are taken into account and the team is committed to the process. The increased participation, commitment and productivity achieved by this approach justifies the re-evaluation of more traditional performance appraisal systems currently being used.

Although this system appears cumbersome at first glance, the reliability and validity of the appraisal process is improved because of the increased understanding and commitment of team members. To us it appears that 360 degree goal setting and appraisal is a human resource tool which has tremendous potential for IT in the 1990s.

Steps in Coaching and Counseling

The person in "charge" formerly had unquestioned authority to command and compel. In the learning organization, managers must focus on persuading rather than ordering workers to perform. Managers must learn to coach employees to achieve their goals and change their behavior to be more effective in teams. How can the IT manager do this effectively? One of the best ways is through feedback and counseling.

Giving Feedback. Managers can provide two kinds of feedback: general feedback and feedback on goal accomplishment. The following incident is an example of a manager providing poor general feedback, yet she is effective at feedback on goal accomplishment. Tom, an individual contributor working in a IT department, submits a request to attend a new client-server seminar. His manager, Kathy, receives the request but forgets about it and never gets back to Tom. On the other hand, Kathy excels at goal accomplishment feedback because she gives Tom specific feedback about his progress on personal and strategic goals throughout the year and during his annual review. What Kathy may not realize is one of the most effective ways managers can make work more meaningful, is not only to give Tom more feedback on his goals, but also to follow-up on his other needs such as general feedback.

Feedback and the Self-Concept. In the example above, Tom has a self-concept that was developed over years and years of conditioning. Out of that conditioning process comes attitudes, feelings, and behavior. The self-concept is very delicate and any feedback that is perceived as negative or damaging can be rejected by the individual contributor. Some general rules for giving feedback are:

1. Give people timely feedback. Make certain that your feedback follows the desired or undesired behavior as soon as possible. If you go on a trip or get too busy to give immediate feedback, first evaluate whether the feedback is still appropriate. If you decide it is, you should do two things: first apologize for the delay and, second, do your best to recreate the situation so the feedback is more meaningful. During the feed-

back session look for signals that indicate the person under-stands the feedback and is willing to change his behavior. Once you see this understanding and acknowledgment, don't dwell on the point.

2. Jointly develop an action plan to change behavior. This will ensure a greater degree of commitment to the action plan by the person who has the undesired behavior. Take great care to be consistent in your feedback. Studies show that the likeli-hood of change is directly related to the consistency of feed-back. Set a date to review the person's progress on any action plans you jointly establish. Then, make sure you follow through with a follow-up session. Not following through can be worse then not addressing the undesired behavior.

3. At the follow-up session, discuss the person's progress on the action plan. Look for feedback from the person's peers re-garding any noticeable change in behavior. Then, you com-pliment the individual on any positive changes in behavior. If the individual has changed his behavior and his peers do not give him credit for it, encourage the individual to continue the new behavior and give the change process more time. Re-search indicates there is a lag between the actual change in behavior and recognition by peers by as much as six months. Figure 5-4 is a checklist of the steps in the feedback process.

We recommend you review the previous steps before any feed-back sessions with your people. You may even desire to keep a list on these feedback guidelines on your desk or on a bulletin board near your desk. Professional counselors generally agree that the above guidelines are the basic sequence of steps for help-ing a person improve their problem-solving behavior and for con-ducting a joint goal setting session. By following these steps care-fully, coaches and managers can increase the employee's general satisfaction.

Helpful Hints for the Session. While the above guidelines are more general, there are specific rules for the actual face-to-face meeting. By reviewing these rules before the session, the meeting can move through an orderly process toward joint solu-

1. Present criticism in a way that allows others to improve their behavior.

2. Comment only on behavior people can change.

3. Give timely feedback.

4. Look for signals indicating the person understands your feedback and is willing to change the behavior.

5. Be consistent in your feedback.

6. Jointly develop an action plan to change the undesired behavior.

7. Set a date to review the action plan you establish, then follow through.

8. Discuss progress on the action plan during the follow-up session.

9. Encourage the person to continue the change process, even if peers do not recognize the behavior change.

10. Develop an atmosphere where peers may exchange feedback.

11. Keep telling your employees that you appreciate their high performance.

Figure 5-4. Steps in the Feedback Process.

tions which will benefit the individual, the team, and the organization. The steps are:

1. Setting the stage. Explain the purpose of the session, what the outcome will look like, and that the session is not to torture the individual contributor, but a joint goal setting session to increase the learning process.

2. Interaction. Develop and follow an action plan, so all ideas on the agenda are discussed logically and as completely as

necessary. The coach should do at least fifty percent of the listening.

3. Control the session. Stay on target and move toward specific objectives for the session. Develop an atmosphere of sharing responsibility for resolving the problems under discussion.

4. Tone of the session. Candid and open communication establishes a climate that is helpful, supportive, and productive. Don't allow threats, shouting, tirades, or recriminations.

5. Joint solutions. Look for answers to causes of the problems, not superficial treatment of the symptoms. Make the process a joint discovery between the two of you.

6. Joint goal setting. The goal should be challenging yet reachable in a reasonable time frame. Help the person set priorities and allocate resources to help the individual reach the target.

7. Follow up. Set a date to check on progress and, if necessary, select alternative goals or alternative actions to the previously established objectives. Make changes in goals as necessary to keep the person on track and responsible for changing the undesired behavior.

Summary and Conclusions

The search for the ideal goal setting and performance appraisal system is a continuous journey that moves from traditional appraisal systems to collaborative systems, and now to 360 degree processes. The evolution of performance appraisal systems will not end with 360 degree appraisal because, although this system has many advantages, it also has numerous disadvantages. Thus, the search for the *perfect system* will continue. In the interim, 360 degree goal setting and appraisal is the best system for the organization of the future (STAR).[4]

Probably the easiest mistake to make when designing a 360 degree goal setting and performance appraisal process is trying to include too broad of an internal and external customer base. Remember your core business! Although providing clear goals is extremely important it can be a balancing act between an effective goal setting process and one which turns into an administrative nightmare. Finally, keep the process flexible to accommodate a changing and learning organization.

References

1. O'Reilly, Brian. "360-Feedback Can Change Your Life". **Fortune**. Oct. 17, 1994.

2. John F. Milliman, Robert A. Zawacki, Carol A. Norman, Lynda Powell and Jay Kirksey, "Companies Evaluate Employees From All Perspectives," **Personnel Journal**, November, 1994, pp. 99-103 and Robert A. Zawacki, T. A. Mills and Nick Pile, "360 Degree Performance Appraisal in IT," **The Software Practitioner**, November, 1994, pages 14-15.

3. Carol A. Norman and Robert A. Zawacki, "Team Appraisals-Team Approach," **Personnel Journal**, September, 1991, pages 101-104.

4. John F. Milliman, Robert A. Zawacki, Sally Wiggins, Carol A. Norman, "Customer Driven Goal Setting," Research report submitted to **Personnel Journal**, accepted for publication during 1995.

Chapter 6

Selecting People for the STAR Organization

Introduction

As information technology budgets continue to decrease, as IT organizations continue to reduce their headcount, and as they are subjected to ever increasing pressure by CEOs to demonstrate value added, there is an increasing need for IT leaders to select people who are motivated to be extremely productive. Although IT leaders will invest in new hardware and software to increase productivity, our research indicates IT leaders are reluctant to invest in a selection system that will increase productivity through the better match-up of people and jobs.

Further, people make up approximately fifty percent of the typical IT budget, and although there will continue to be increases in productivity through the application of better hardware and software, the largest increases in productivity will come from the human side of IT during the 1990s.

In addition to the need to match people better with jobs, another need of organizations is to select leaders for the STAR organization, who not only have excellent technical skills, but are also excellent coaches. This transformation from manager to coach can be accelerated through the use of assessment centers.

Ability, Motivation, and the Job Itself

Three variables predict effective job performance for an information technology professional.[1] The variables are ability, motivation, and the job itself. Figure 6-1 diagrams this relationship between the variables.

Ability includes the candidate's job experience and technical ability, skill level, aptitude, and education. Motivation is the candidate's drive to achieve and the job consists of the five core job dimensions which are: skill variety, task identity, task significance, autonomy, and feedback. Motivation (growth need strength)

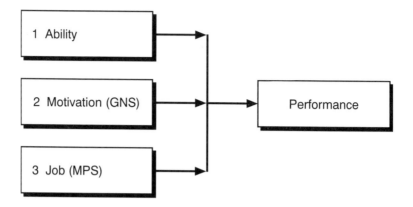

Figure 6-1. Determinants of Employee Performance.

and the job itself (motivating potential score) were discussed extensively in Chapter 3.

Interviewing People. Our research indicates that IT leaders tend to overhire for the job. That is, they tend to hire very high growth need strength people (GNS) and then place them in a job with low motivating potential (MPS). What exactly happens during the interview process?

During the 1980s we did extensive research on the joining-up process used in typical IT organizations and the results were published in **Computerworld** and **Datamation**. The primary findings of our research and the research of others are:[2]

> All available research indicates that the ability of an IT leader to predict how a future employee will perform, based upon a one hour interview, is very low. Yet most IT leaders have great confidence in their predictive ability based upon impressions formed in a brief interview. Why is there a discrepancy between a manager's belief about his or her predictive ability and our research results? There are two main reasons for this belief:

> 1. *The person being interviewed tends to give socially desirable answers to the interviewer.* Assume a systems analyst desperately wants a job at ITT Hartford because of the poor employment situation on the East Coast of the United States. The candidate can prepare for the interview by studying ITT

Hartford's financial reports, become familiar with their products, technology, and even talk to other systems analysts at the company. Further, many IT managers are very busy and do not prepare for the interview and tend to "wing it." In a one-hour interview, the odds are in the candidates favor that they will get the job.

2. *The Interviewer's biases are based on a poor research methodology.* In the example above, assume the interviewer talked to five candidates for the systems analysis job. After interviewing all five candidates, the interviewer selects the person who interviewed "the best" or was rated the highest. This candidate then joins ITT Hartford and is an above average employee for the next three years. The interviewer's impressions about his ability to predict effective future job performance is reinforced because the interviewer only sees the positive results of the interview. What the interviewer does not know is how the other four candidates would have performed. They could have gone to Aetna, Travelers, or Cigna and done outstanding work and be superior to the person hired by ITT Hartford. Thus, the research methodology used by the typical interviewer is fraught with errors.

3. Some additional research findings are:

   a. Interviewers tend to develop a stereotype of a good candidate and then seem to match applicants with stereotypes. During our joining-up research we actually observed an interviewer who had a personal pilot's license and noticed from the candidate's vita that the candidate also had a pilot's license. During the interview, the two people only talked about flying, yet the interviewer recommended the IT firm hire the candidate. This is the ultimate in stereotyping - a good pilot is a good programmer!

   b. Biases are established early in the interview process.

   c. During an interview in which the applicant is

accepted, the interviewer talks more often and in a more favorable tone than in an interview in which the applicant is rejected. If the interviewer likes the candidate, the questions become easier to answer and are presented in a more friendly manner. If the interviewer develops an unfavorable impression of the candidate, the questions become harder and more direct, thus giving a signal to the candidate.

d. Interviewing negative candidates before positive candidates will result in a greater number of favorable acceptances than the other way around. Thus, the interview changes the standard for selection because of the need for closure and to get back to more important things, such as technical issues.

e. There are reliable and consistent individual differences among interviewers in their perceptions of the applicants they see as acceptable. These perceptions of differences can be very positive for the IT organization if there is a follow-up meeting of the interviewers to discuss the candidates. Our research indicates many IT organizations skip the follow-up meeting because of time constraints and their desire not to attend meetings.

f. Factual written data seems to be more important than physical appearance in determining judgments; this increases with interviewing experience.

g. Early impressions by the typical interviewer are crystallized after a mean interview time of only four minutes. This finding is especially damaging for IT leaders because of their high growth need strength and heavy demands on their schedule. They have a natural tendency to make quick decisions and tend to resist using the full time set aside for the interview. Our research further indicates that over sixty percent of IT interviewers have made up their minds about the desirability of the candidate after 20 minutes into the interview process. For an interview to be effective (valid) it takes from 15 to 20 minutes just to establish rapport between the interviewer and the candidate. Thus, this is one of the primary reasons why the predictive ability of the interview is very low.

h. The ability of a candidate to respond concisely, to answer questions fully, to state personal opinions when relevant, and to keep to the subject at hand appears to be crucial to obtaining a favorable employment decision.

i. Interviewers benefit very little from day-to-day interviewing experience unless they participate in a post interviewing focus group which helps the interviewers learn from their collective experiences.

j. An interviewer who begins an interview with an unfavorable expectancy may tend to give the candidate less credit for past accomplishments and ultimately may be more likely to decide that the applicant is unacceptable.

k. There are three types of interview formats which are: structured or patterned, unstructured or nondirective and the problem interview. The research clearly indicates that the structured interview, with proper training, is the best format. Figure 6-2 contains the guidelines for a structured or patterned interview.

Changing Competencies. As IT leaders transform their organizations, they should also consider the competencies which will be required in the STAR organization. In addition to technical skills, future individual contributors will need consulting, ne-

1. Preparing for the interview:
   a. Arrange for a comfortable physical environment.
   b. Get away from the telephone and interruptions.
   c. Clear your mind of organizational problems and review these guidelines.
   d. Write down four or five open ended questions that will help you evaluate the candidate's growth need strength (GNS), skills, and other technical competencies.
   e. Review the job descriptions and determine the scope of the job (MPS). Remember, select a high GNS person for a job, such as development, that will motivate them over time.
   f. Review the candidate's resume.

2. Structuring the interview:
   a. Use multiple interviewers in succession; this increases the predictive validity of the joining-up process.
   b. Keep short notes of each interview.
   c. Ask each candidate the same questions.

3. Conducting the interview:
   a. Greet the candidate in a friendly manner. The opening minutes of the interview process are critical because both the candidate and the interviewer are forming impressions.
   b. Establish rapport and trust by discussing a common point of interest. Determine this from the candidate's resume. After about 15 minutes you must move on to more technical questions.
   c. Be aware of your facial expressions. Talk in a relaxed manner and attempt to smile.
   d. Conduct the interview face-to-face. Do not have a desk or table between yourself and the candidate.
   e. Start with broad general questions to relax the candidate and then proceed to the technical questions.
   f. Ask open ended questions that permit the candidate to do at least fifty percent of the talking. For example, a poor question is: Did you graduate from a software engineering program? A better way to word it would be: Please tell me about your college courses and experiences.
   g. Give positive strokes to the candidate when possible. For example, You completed a very complex and innovative project when you worked at TTI.
   h. Use pauses to your advantage to keep the candidate talking.

Figure 6-2. Guidelines for the Structured or Patterned Interview.

i. Observe time limits and bring the interview to a polite close. For example, I find your work experience very interesting, I would love to talk to you more but I must keep you on schedule and introduce you to the next interviewer.

j. End the interview by telling the candidate the time schedule for hiring and when and who will get back to them. Remember, the best candidates have the most opportunities.

k. Escort the candidate to the next interviewer, introduce the candidate, and thank them for their time and interest.

4. **After the interview:**
   a. Make notes about the candidate while impressions are fresh on your mind.
   b. Schedule a meeting with the other interviewers to compare and discuss all the candidates. This meeting should take place immediately after the last interview.
   c. Call the successful candidate immediately after the hiring decision. Follow-up with a letter to the unsuccessful candidates. Besides the consideration of common decency, remember that rejected candidates talk to other people about how they were treated by your organization and people buy products - they are the customer!

Figure 6-2 continued. Guidelines for the Structured or Patterned Interview.

gotiation, and conflict resolution skills. As we indicated in Chapter 3, our research indicates that IT organizations have a large percentage of their people with low social need strength (SNS). Low SNS people are less effective working with customers because they do not naturally possess a high need for interaction with other people, and learning the people skills is not a motivator. They prefer to learn about new technology and leave the people skills to others. Because this low SNS is a major problem in almost all IT organizations, we researched the behaviors of people low in SNS and those high in SNS. Those behaviors are listed in Figure 6-3.

Individual Contributor's Name _____

Firm or Organization _____ Date _____

Definition of Need for Affilition: Also referred to as Social Need Strength (SNS), it is a measure of a person's need to have meaningful interpersonal relationships, both on and off the job. A person with high SNS usually is more motivated to meet with customers, has better negotiation, conflict resolution, and change skills, and is more willing to learn these competencies.

DETERMINING SNS

Using the scale below, rate the person on each dimension of SNS with 1 being low and 7 being high. Total the dimensions and divide by 7. The result is your estimate of the person's SNS.

1. Does not join or   Joins activities
   attend activities   and attends

   Low   Average   High

   1   2   3   4   5   6   7   [   ]

2. Works alone   Teamworker

   Low   Average   High

   1   2   3   4   5   6   7   [   ]

3. Does not help others   Is willing to help others

   Low   Average   High

   1   2   3   4   5   6   7   [   ]

4. Unwilling to adapt   Willing to adapt

   Low   Average   High

   1   2   3   4   5   6   7   [   ]

Figure 6-3. Need For Affiliation (SNS).

5. Few contacts   Many contacts

    Low   Average   High

    1   2   3   4   5   6   7

6. Week feedback   Seeks and gives feedback

    Low   Average   High

    1   2   3   4   5   6   7

7. Seldom seen   Highly visible

    Low   Average   High

    1   2   3   4   5   6   7

Individual SNS is computed by totaling the ratings and dividing by seven.
Round to one decimal place.

Total Score of Ratings 1 thru 7		SNS is: Total Score ÷ 7	

Figure 6-3 continued. Need For Affiliation (SNS). *

* Readers of this book are free to copy this SNS form to use in their joining-up process. If you desire professional copies please telephone 719 599-0849. Copies of Form SNS are $2.00 each in lots of 100 plus shipping charges.

Selecting People For the Future. In addition to selecting people who have superior technical ability, the future IT organization will hire and train people to work in teams, work with customers, and some of them will eventually become coaches for teams. Therefore, IT leaders must develop a dual strategy to hire and train their people for the future STAR organization.

The first strategy is to select people with high growth need strength (GNS) and high need for affiliation (SNS). Figure 6-4 is a modification of Figure 6-1 and we recommend this as a model when interviewing people for jobs requiring consulting and negotiation skills.

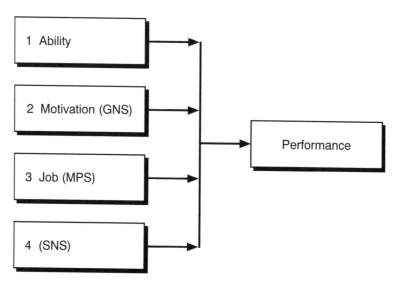

Figure 6-4. Determinants of Employee Performance for Interfacing Jobs.

The second approach is to provide training in consulting skills and negotiation skills for your existing software engineers who will work in the business units or with the business units. Hewlett-Packard recognized the changing role of IT and they responded with a training program for the *fast track* software engineers which they titled the IT Business Process Consultant. The objective of the program is to develop a cadre of process experts within the IT function who are able to play a full partner role in major business process enhancement and innovation. H-P believes the competencies needed by these people are: project management, business process skills, planning and architecture, consulting, and system integration.

To accomplish its objectives, H-P designed a five-block program that was taught with internal and external resources. The program was designed with a six-week break between blocks where the students were given an assignment to apply their knowledge in their project work in their IT organization and then they returned and shared their learning with other class members. This combination of blocks of instruction, reinforced with learning by doing, and then discussing what was learned proved very successful at H-P.

Another IT organization that recognized the need for business process and consulting skills was United Technologies Carrier Information Systems. They decided to use a training strategy to help their people acquire skills in the following areas: program management, business strategy, consulting and change management. Using internal and external resources, they designed a three-day program that was based upon the recognition that their people had very high growth need strength and below average social need strength. Thus, they recognized that they had to develop commitment to the training program by creating *need awareness for negotiating and consulting training.*

The program began with an unfreezing process that included many exercises designed to understand better the changing role of IT and the competencies required to partner with the business units to add value to the bottom line. After this unfreezing process, the systems people acquired actual negotiation skills through role playing and the final block of the course was an assignment that required them to use these new skills as soon as possible. Finally, Carrier's IT leadership team is working on a reward system to reinforce this new behavior.

Finding People with Consulting Skills

Organizations that place a high value on selecting the right people and developing them to be high performers often use assessment centers. Assessment centers are a tool that have tremendous potential for selecting people with consulting and negotiation skills, who can work in teams, and evaluate the potential for people to be coaches of self directed teams. Assessment centers were used extensively in the early 1960s by AT&T in its Bell System companies before the firm was broken up. Assessment centers are now beginning to receive renewed attention because of the need to select people who are more adaptable to change and willing to prepare themselves to work in the organization of the future.[3]

The advantage of the assessment center over the interview is that the candidate's behavior can be observed. The disadvantages are the large time commitments, the need for an extensive design, and the obvious cost considerations. Potential candidates for a job are asked to attend an off-site assignment which is typically two to three days in length. At the session, the candidates are interviewed, given a series of aptitude and skill tests, participate in a leaderless group exercise, and write a summary of a business case. Typically, the evaluation of the candidates is done by managers and individual contributors from the organization.

Examples of Assessment Centers. Hamilton Standard Commercial Aircraft Electronics Division of United Technologies (HSCAE) designed a very flat organization based on self directed teams to produce jet engine control systems for the Boeing 777. Because of the need to manufacture low volumes of high quality products, the company decided to design an assessment center that met two critical conditions: (1) current team members needed to be involved in the selection process, and (2) the program needed to assess each individual's ability to work in teams in addition to a high level of technical skills.

To meet these requirements, the company implemented a multistep assessment program. The steps are: (1) an information session for people who submit resumes, (2) at the end of the information session, people are invited to complete job applications, (3) invited candidates, in groups of about 70 people, are evaluated for one day, and (4) candidates are given aptitude tests, technical tests, and evaluated for their ability to work in teams. After the above steps, all hiring decisions are made by group consensus. After two years, the assessment program is judged as a success because customer relations have improved and quality is up with lowering marketing costs.

The assessment center concept has tremendous potential to evaluate candidates to be coaches in self directed teams. One major East Coast financial institution decided to transform its IT organization from a top-down hierarchy to a team based organization. To accomplish this goal, it evaluated its present managers' ability to transition into coaching roles using the desirable qualities of a team coordinator. The team coordinator duties were described in Chapter 4 and are displayed in Figure 6-5.

Competency	Low			Level			High	My Score
	1	2	3	4	5	6	7	
1. Mentor/Coach								
2. Flexibility								
3. Deals with Change								
4. Facilitator								
5. Values People and Tasks								
6. Listener								
7. Negotiator								
8. General Knowledge of Technical and Business Areas								
9. Problem Solver								
10. Organized								
11. Shared Control								
12. Lead by Example								
13. Trust Building Skills								
14. Provides for Career Development								
15. Open Communication-Sharing Information with the Team								

My Personal Improvement Goals:
Name: _____ Date: _____
1.
2.

Figure 6-5. Desirable Qualities of a Team Coordinator.

The IT organization formed an assessment center team which had representation from senior management, middle management, human resources, and the advice of an outside organizational consultant. All current first-line managers were asked to be evaluated and agreed to participate in the assessment. First, the organizational consultant interviewed each manager extensively. Next, each manager was interviewed by the assessment team and each team member rated the candidates on the scale in Figure 6-5. Finally, the team met and discussed each candidates' ability to make the transition from a top-down control model to a coaching model. The results of the exercise was that the assessment team recommended that fifty percent of the managers could make the transition. This selection percentage agrees with the research on self directed teams.[4]

After the evaluation and notification of the candidates, the people who could not make the transition into a coaching role, were given the opportunity to receive training and again become individual contributors as PC LAN programmers, systems analysts or database administrators.

One person, who was a high performer as a traditional manager, objected to the assessment team's decision and asked the senior vice president for I/S to give him an opportunity to demonstrate his ability to be a coach. After much counsel and thought, the senior vice president placed the former manager in charge of a development team. After six months in a shared governance role (coaching), the traditional manager asked to become an individual contributor and his desire was honored. In addition to working with the traditional manager toward becoming a coach, another benefit of this failure was that it demonstrated to the other members of the organization that failure was all right, if they can learn from their mistakes. Thus, IT leadership began to introduce the learning organization.

Another example of the effective use of the assessment concept is the information systems department of a major international manufacturing company. Their IT leadership team determined, with the assistance of their human resources department, that in addition to technical skills, their first-line managers need to be adaptable to change. After reviewing the research literature, they designed and implemented the evaluation form displayed in Figure 6-6.

This IT organization implemented a posting of all openings

1. SELF AWARENESS
    Low   High
    1   2   3   4   5   6   7

2. FLEXIBILITY
                                                              Very
    Inflexible   Flexible
    1   2   3   4   5   6   7

3. RESOURCEFULNESS
    Low   High
    1   2   3   4   5   6   7

4. DOES WHAT IT TAKES
    Low Energy   High Energy
    and Drive   and Drive
    1   2   3   4   5   6   7

5. GRASP OF THE SITUATION
    Slow to   Quick
    Learn   Study
    1   2   3   4   5   6   7

Name: _____ My Score: _____

Date: _____

    Key:
              30-35   Very adaptable to change
              25-29   Adaptable to change
              24 and below   Need training

Figure 6-6. Adaptability/Change Index.

for first-line management jobs and the notice included instructions that anyone could apply for the job and would be evaluated
by an assessment center. The assessment center had a standing
team that served for two years and met twice a year to evaluate
candidates. The team rated each candidate and then held a private
meeting where they discussed each candidate and asked the person who rated the candidate the lowest and the person who rated
the candidate the highest, to share their evaluation and reasons
with the assessment team. This process permitted the negatives
and the positives to be discussed before team members firmed up

their individual ratings and the team arrived at a group consensus. Also, this evaluation process became the basis for a developmental plan for the people who were not selected to be first-line managers.

Summary and Conclusions

The Need For Affiliation (SNS) Form, Desirable Qualities of a Team Coordinator Form, and Adaptability/Change Index can be used in any combination. The key to a successful joining-up process is to determine the competencies that your IT organization will need in the future. Once that determination is made, then set up a structured interviewing program, that not only evaluates the candidate's core technical competencies, but also evaluates the candidate's potential for success when consulting with the business units. Further, seriously consider implementing an assessment center to evaluate each individual contributor's ability to become a consultant and adjust to random change. Also, evaluate your first-line managers' ability to become coaches and change champions. Finally, your performance appraisal and reward systems must be designed to evaluate and reinforce consulting, change, and coaching skills. Behaviors which are rewarded are repeated!

References

1. Robert A. Zawacki, "Ability, Motivation, and the Job Itself: What is the Relationship?" **Managing System Development**, June, 1993, pages 8-9.

2. Robert A. Zawacki, "MIS Struggles to Hire Wisely," **Computerworld**, May 25, 1987, pages 73-74 and Robert A. Zawacki, "How to Pick Eagles," **Datamation**, September 15, 1985, pages 115-116. Also see Abraham K. Korman, **Industrial and Organizational Psychology** (Englewood Cliffs, N.J.: Prentice-Hall, 1971) and Wayne F. Cascio, **Applied Psychology in Personnel Management** (Reston, VA.: Reston Publishing Co., 1982).

3. Jay Kirksey and Robert A. Zawacki, "Assessment Center Helps Find Team-Oriented Candidates," **Personnel Journal**, May, 1994, page 92.

4. Robert A. Zawacki, "Do I/S and Teams Mix?" **Computerworld**, June 13, 1994, page 122.

PART III

LINKING STRUCTURE, MOTIVATION, AND CHANGE MANAGEMENT WITH INFORMATION TECHNOLOGY AND BUSINESS RESULTS

Chapter 7

Transforming the Mature IT Organization: A Balanced Implementation Approach

Introduction

This chapter extends the thesis previously presented by introducing a balanced approach to transforming the IT organization. The summary chapter of the book includes a discussion of business effectiveness, technology effectiveness, and functional effectiveness of IT organizations.

Although today's tenets such as the learning organization, the changing core competencies, organizational architecture, the horizontal organization, business process reengineering, time based competition, and value based competition are all based on sound management theory, most efforts in these tenets are failing as IT leaders attempt to add value to the bottom line of the business, reduce staff, flatten the organization, start teams, and at the same time maintain, or even increase, customer service and productivity.

Management tenets can contribute to the bottom line; however, the real gains in customer service and productivity come from a balanced implementation approach that is based upon the STAR organization of the future which is designed for this decade of high velocity change.

Assumptions About Change

One of the main reasons for lack of effective change is that many IT leaders may be making the wrong assumptions about change. IT professionals have experienced two different change paradigms and continue to "hang on to" those paradigms. The truth is that those two paradigms are no longer relevant for our fast-changing environment which is currently locked in time and value based competition.

Tell and Sell. First, when more effective and ever-larger mainframes were introduced in the 1950's and 1960's, information systems people viewed technological change as incremental, they adapted, and stayed ahead of the rate of change. Information systems people were in control, told the business units what they needed and when they would get it. We call this period of incremental change "the tell and sell approach." Some consequences of this "tell and sell approach" were: IT managers viewed themselves as the experts on information technology within the organization and the business should (and did) come to them for advice, and there was a slowly developing negative view of IT organizations by the business units. The business leaders began to view IT as not understanding the business and not meeting the business needs in a timely and cost effective manner.

Rapid Change. In the 1970's and 1980's, we entered the second period of change which was more "rapid." As change became more rapid, IT people still stayed ahead of the change curve by working harder (average hours worked per week is still increasing in America), working smarter (just-in-time inventories processes, etc.), and introducing more technologies such as midrange computers, microcomputers, LANS, WANS, and client-server. During this second period of rapid change, customers became more computer literate, software became more user friendly, and the customer became more vocal about the effectiveness of IT. Further, the shared influence between the customer and IT increased and, in some organizations, even reached the state of a true partnership.

Random Change. In the current paradigm, change is now random and appears to lack cause and effect from the point of view of the individual contributor. In previous periods of incremental and rapid change, there was a cause and effect. For example, the individual contributor went to a good university, graduated with a degree in computer science, joined the firm as a junior programmer, and advanced through system analyst to manager. Thus, individual contributors could clearly distinguish the relationship between their high performance and rewards. However, during random change, the consequences of hard work are more difficult, or even impossible, to determine as organizations downsized based on the life cycle of a project rather than individual performance.

An example of lack of cause and effect during this period of random change is that of a recent graduate of a major university. She joined a leading hardware company as a software engineer, worked hard for eight years, obtained outstanding performance appraisals and above average salary increases, and thought she was on the fast track. As the company began to experience declining market share and profit margins, staff was reduced significantly. Finally, in desperation, management closed down the product line she was working on and she was forced into a buy-out and left the firm. To the person in this situation, the world seems to lack cause and effect.

The Mandate for Transformation

Many IT leaders are still working in or designing change programs for the paradigms of the past four decades (incremental and rapid change) which are doomed to failure because the remainder of the organization is subjected to the extreme turbulence of today's business world caused by *continuous discontinuous* change. It is becoming widely accepted that the countless business process redesign projects underway in organizations around the world need to be much more than one time events to achieve their objectives. The philosophy of continuous improvement of business processes is rapidly being adopted as a fundamental strategy in response to the random change character of today's business environment. This accelerating movement has enormous implications for IT organizations.

No Longer Business as Usual. With organizational mandates continuously to improve business processes, IT organizations can no longer take a "business as usual" approach in support of their business customers. To do so invites increased criticism for lack of responsiveness as traditional IT operating methods simply cannot keep pace with the required time frame of continuous improvement.

Adding to the challenges facing IT organizations is the accelerating pace of new technology, the skill sets required to gain the benefits of such technology, and the quagmire of legacy systems. To meet successfully such challenges, IT organizations must change in three central areas: the way they relate to other business units, the way new technology is deployed, and in the way IT professionals are organized, evaluated, and acquire new skill sets. In short, today's challenges require a transformation of IT organizations.

Outsourcing Distributed Systems. The transformation mandate cannot be ignored. IT leaders will either implement effective transformation programs for their organizations or they will suffer through a series of endless initiatives to improve IT responsiveness, many of which will be led or sponsored by their business customers. The growing trend of outsourcing distributed systems provides evidence of the latter response. It was recently reported that U.S. firms will have spent $1.3 billion for such outsourcing in 1994 and are expected to increase annual spending for distributed system outsourcing to $6.4 billion in five years. The leading reasons given for these expenditures included implementation of new technology, improving support, and improving productivity. Cost reduction was ranked last.[1] Such actions merely shift a portion of the transformation responsibilities to outsiders and may, in fact, make the transformation journey more difficult.

A Balanced Approach to Transformation

We propose a transformation approach that balances efforts directed toward increasing the business effectiveness, technology effectiveness, and functional effectiveness of the IT organization. Actions in the business effectiveness arena are designed to translate overall business strategies into operational directions for IT. Technology effectiveness deals with how new technologies can be deployed to provide maximum benefit with minimum disruption to the organization. Functional effectiveness addresses the organization structure, operating methods, and personnel development required for IT organizations to deliver valued services in the present decade of random change. The degree of effort should be applied in each of these three broad categories will vary, depending on current strengths and weaknesses of the IT organization. However, we have yet to see a situation which did not require attention directed toward certain elements within each category.

Business Effectiveness. We have identified three principal drivers of IT business effectiveness: strong goal alignment between IT and individual business units, work redesign to take advantage of the new technologies, and leadership development to provide capable executive sponsorship for IT initiatives.

Alignment of IT transformation objectives with organizational goals is a fundamental requirement for success in an age of random change. While "meeting business needs" has long been recognized as an important central objective for IT organizations, the business impact of IT support was seen over a longer time span prior to the era of random change. Thus, IT leaders had time to compensate for lack of effective goal alignment with their business customers.

Random change has eliminated this compensation time and has made the pain of poor alignment almost immediate. Now, more than ever, IT leaders must be unyielding in their efforts to ensure their initiatives are precisely focused on the highest priorities of their business unit customers.

All too often we hear business unit executives make the statement that they have no alternative other than to initiate projects on their own to meet their needs for more responsive systems. Such was the case in a major high technology company whose director of information systems maintained that the role of the IT organization was to tell the users "what systems they would get and when they would get them." As a result, a major conflict arose when the chief financial officer, who desperately needed new systems to manage the explosive growth of the organization, initiated an effort to select new financial software. The result of this struggle was further isolation of the IT organization from the other business units.

An example of a more positive response to the realities of today's high velocity environment is seen in the IT organization of a major computer manufacturer. In this case, IT leadership recognized that new skill sets were required to serve their business customers better. Accordingly, formal programs were established to select and train IT professionals to become "business consultants." The focus of this program was to partner IT professionals with their business unit customers to address specific business problems and to reduce the organization's reliance on out-side consultants.

Many times IT leaders treat goal alignment efforts as a one-time event conducted during annual budgeting activities. Such an approach ignores the random change nature of the business environment. Effective goal alignment requires establishment of on-going processes to maintain a proper focus of IT activities when dealing with a dynamic environment.

A very powerful way to establish and sustain strong goal alignment is through work redesign. IT leaders have significant responsibilities and opportunities in business process reengineering and continuous improvement initiatives. Principal responsibilities include gaining a thorough appreciation of the operating environment and key success factors of their business customers, and understanding the capabilities and limitations of new technologies. Participation, as part of work restructuring teams, presents unparalleled opportunities for IT professionals to demonstrate their value to the organization and to build strong working relationships with key personnel in the business units.

IT leaders must ensure that business process improvement teams are provided with complete and accurate information regarding the potential of new technologies to support process improvement. Today's desktop and client-server based technologies provide IT professionals with an unprecedented opportunity to enable process improvements. Object-oriented, workflow-based system development environments and application software, such as that to be provided by KaPRE Software, have significant potential to support radically different work processes and continuous improvement initiatives. IT professionals should gain a solid understanding of the capabilities of such new technologies and bring this knowledge to the process improvement teams.

Participation in process improvement teams by well prepared IT professionals provides a clear focus for technology initiatives and identifies the business unit sponsors required to successfully achieve the full benefits of such initiatives. IT leaders should view business process improvement initiatives as opportunities to validate continuously their transformation action plans and strengthen support for their transformation journey.

Change at a Pharmaceutical Company. An example of

strong participation by IT in business process improvement efforts is seen in a major pharmaceutical manufacturer. Senior management of the organization determined that the company must transform itself from a group of independent business units operating in various countries around the world to a true *global organization*. A key enabler of this transformation was the implementation of common financial and manufacturing systems in all locations.

Management correctly recognized that the business process improvement efforts associated with the system implementations were only the first step in their transformation journey. To support continuous improvement activities, resource centers were established on both an area (Europe, North America, and Asia) and a global basis. The resource centers were staffed with professionals from IT as well as the business units. The charter of the resource centers included providing specialized skills in the areas of project management, business process improvement, information technology, and management of organizational change, in addition to specific support roles for the new financial and manufacturing systems.

The third component of business effectiveness is establishment of capable executive sponsorship for IT initiatives. Business unit executive sponsors are readily available for IT projects driven from business process improvement initiatives. However, a common weakness we have observed in many companies which can quickly undermine the business effectiveness of an IT organization is the assumption that executives have the necessary skills to provide required sponsorship of IT projects. All too often we see senior management members willingly accept the role of executive sponsor and think their responsibility ends at that point, or they know they should be doing more, but they are clue-less regarding what they should be doing. In such instances, leadership development and coaching initiatives should be implemented by the IT leadership team.

The typical focus required in leadership development programs for executive sponsors of IT projects is on the sponsorship role in managing organizational change. It is very difficult for information technology transformation initiatives to succeed without addressing organizational change issues from the senior levels within the organization. The first step to becoming an effective executive sponsor is gaining an understanding of the concepts of change management, why people resist positive as well as negative change, and what roles are required of executive management and senior IT leaders to overcome resistance to change.

When the fundamental concepts of managing organizational change are understood, efforts should be directed toward identification of specific areas of resistance to change and development of distinct action plans to overcome such resistance. These plans should become an integral part of the overall system implementation plan.

Technology Effectiveness. We characterize technology effectiveness as the deployment of new technologies in a manner that delivers maximum benefits with a minimum of organizational disruption. To achieve this objective, we have found specific strategies for technology evaluation, system implementation and use of outside resources are required.

The rapid advance of new technologies and continuous introduction of methods to extend the utility of older technology requires a focused effort on technology evaluation and selection. For many years technology has been promoted as the enabler of process change and strategic advantage. However, only recently have technologies come on the market which truly support process change without massive expenditures of time and money. As discussed earlier, object-oriented systems just now emerging on the market have significant potential to deliver unparalleled business value.

Now, more than ever, IT leaders should employ dedicated efforts to understand the capabilities of emerging technologies and follow structured evaluation processes to determine the potential of specific technologies to their business customers. Such efforts are also required to determine changes that should be made in system implementation methods to successfully deploy and support emerging technologies. With these practices in place, IT leaders are well positioned to bring the required technological vision to continuous improvement initiatives.

Technology Driven Change. An example of a successful initiative is found in a leading manufacturer and marketer of large data storage and retrieval systems. This organization has adopted an object-oriented application development environment, incorporated with new application software, for a pilot project aimed at integrating mission-critical mainframe and desktop computer systems. The company needed a breakthrough solution to tie these systems together and viewed object technology and workflow driven application architecture as the logical starting point.

The first applications will provide message and document communication for new customer system configuration and quote handling applications distributed among Macintosh notebooks in the field, regional Unix servers and a centralized mainframe. The system will enable cross-functional, process-driven data communications for orders and related transactions between the newer platforms and central legacy systems, reducing overall order-processing cycle times and improving cash flow.

The Place for Methodologies? A problem we frequently see which quickly undermines the success of new technology introduction is the assumption that system implementation methodologies, rigidly followed, will lead to success or new technologies do not require the use of implementation methodologies. In fact, some IT experts are proclaiming that methodologies are no longer useful with new technologies.

We have yet to see a methodology containing all the answers to implementation challenges or see a technology implementation effort which could not benefit from methodological support. A common characteristic of successful efforts is use of flexible implementation guidelines, or best practices, that have been adapted to the environment of the project by experienced practitioners and have been combined with sound project management and quality assurance practices. A common characteristic of successful system development efforts is the establishment of a specific approach (methodology) which defines the work products of the effort (deliverables) and provides measures to evaluate quality and progress.

An example of blind adherence to an inappropriate methodology is seen in a major telecommunications company. The company initiated a project to replace its customer information and billing system with new custom developed software using the tools of a leading object software vendor. Much effort was put into development of a new *system develop life cycle* methodology. Unfortunately, the new methodology provided few measurements of quality and progress. After spending over ten million dollars with little to show for it, the project was canceled.

The third dimension of technology effectiveness involves the use of outside assistance. The prudent use of outside resources can be of significant assistance in increasing the technology effectiveness of IT organizations. Many organizations have found the greatest value is received from outside resources when consultants are focused on transferring skills to internal staff members or providing transitional support. In addition to providing best practices for technology implementation, quality assurance, and project management, experienced consultants can provide valuable assistance in legacy system integration and transitional systems outsourcing.

Transitional systems outsourcing is gaining popularity, as it has been successfully used to provide support to legacy systems, which will ultimately be replaced. This approach frees IT personnel from what are generally considered dead end jobs to become proficient in new technologies, which they view as motivational, and to participate in implementation activities.

Functional Effectiveness. We have defined functional effectiveness to include three fundamental organizational attributes required to transform IT organizations: a learning environment, competency development, and benchmarking performance. To provide value in an environment of random change and continuous improvement, IT leaders must give emphasis to placing a high level of importance on each of these areas.

Acquiring new skills has long been a focus of IT professionals and is taken for granted in many organizations. However, to transform successfully an IT organization, the emphasis on learning usually must be increased by one or more orders of magnitude. In short, IT organizations must become *learning organizations* with built-in processes which reflect and gain insights from past outcomes, learn from their mistakes, and disseminate that information to all project leaders. IT leadership must ensure human resource systems and organizational structures are supportive of a learning environment. Initiatives such as 360 degree performance appraisals, technical career tracks, and self directed teams have been found very useful in reinforcing learning environments.

Supporting continuous improvement initiatives and introducing new technologies requires development of new competencies within IT organizations. To add the most value as members of continuous improvement teams, IT professionals must have a fundamental understanding of process reengineering and possess basic consulting skills. These same skills are required to deploy

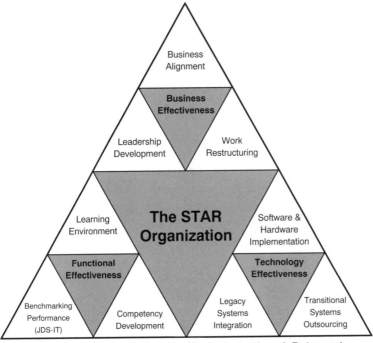

Figure 7-1. Transforming the IT Organization: A Balanced Implementation Approach.

successfully today's emerging technologies. More progressive organizations have recognized the need to develop new competencies and have established consulting career tracks for their IT professionals. Further, the STAR organization of the future must have a true technical career path to motivate systems people as the organization becomes very flat (two layers).

A key success factor in new competency development is the selection of individuals for the initial initiatives and the support and mentoring they receive. We have found benchmarking performance, using measures such as the Job Diagnostic Survey - Information Technology[2], to be very valuable in identification of IT professionals who have a high probability of successfully acquiring the new competencies required for client-server. Such efforts also provide very clear insights regarding the required content of individual development programs. Benchmarking performance also plays a key role in increasing the overall functional effectiveness of IT organizations.

In addition to benchmarking and selecting people who will support the change effort, there is a growing consensus around the fact that the change process can be agonizingly slow, very painful, and IT leaders continuously underestimate the energy required by them to sustain and reinforce the change program.[3] Remember, those new behaviors that are rewarded are repeated!

Summary

The random change embodied in today's business environment, combined with the characteristics and potential of emerging technologies, result in a transformation mandate for IT organizations. To successfully conduct a transformation journey, IT leaders must craft a specific program for their organization that balances the emphasis on individual elements of the transformation model presented above. The effort required in each area will vary from one organization to another. However, it would be a very exceptional organization that could not benefit from some attention in each of the major areas of emphasis.

We designed the STAR organization for the *continuous discontinuous* change of the 1990s. As individuals are exposed to this random change and experience extreme stress, IT leaders of the future must do more than just manage, they must have the coaching and change skills to reenergize the people and the organization. Those IT leaders that can abandon the single-loop skills of the previous four decades, and embrace the concepts of double-loop learning and design a *learning organization* will have a competitive advantage. The learning organization (STAR) is fluid, adaptable and has a built in learning process that permits the people to reflect on their past mistakes, gain insights from those mistakes, and make adjustments to the business processes that truly add value to the bottom-line in this period of high velocity change.

References

1. Bruce Caldwell, "Farming Out Client-Server," **Information Week**, December 12, 1994, pages 46-56.

2. For a complete history of the **Job Diagnostic Survey - Information Technology**, the variables measured, and compared to their international database, write Zawacki and Associates, 7521 Gillen Road, Colorado Springs, CO 80919.

3. Anne B. Fisher, "Making Change Stick,"**Fortune**, April 17, 1995, pages 75-80.

Case 1

Change at the Bank of Ireland With an Outside Change Agent

by T.A. Mills
Partner, KPMG Management Consulting

> Successful delivery of new IT systems is an imperative for financial services companies. Ensuring that an organization is operating 'best practice' in developing its systems offers the surest route to success, given that you are obeying the maxim 'a wise man learns from his mistakes, a wiser man learns from the mistakes of others.'

When the Bank of Ireland decided to improve the performance of the Bank's new systems delivery, they called on KPMG of London for assistance. This case demonstrates the leverage that can be obtained from the effective use of an outside change agent versus an in-house change agent. Some of the advantages of an internal change agent are: (1) familiarity with local jargon and procedures, (2) knowledge of some of the blocks to IT effectiveness, and (3) the fact that the expenses may be less than an external agent's expenses. However, the external change agent has advantages over the internal change agent because: (1) the internal change agent may be part of the problem, (2) the internal change agent may not see the forest for the trees, (3) regardless of the courage and independence of the internal change agent, he is still rewarded by the organization he is trying to change, (4) his fellow IT team members may perceive him as a spy or tool of the boss and he may never have the trust necessary to implement long-term lasting change, and (5) the outside consultant brings with him technical and behavior skills that have been finely tuned in many other change programs.

Conor O'Toole, Head of the Information Systems Department of the Bank of Ireland stated his reasons for using an outside consultant as: "They knew what had to be done and how to do it. They clearly had the methods and techniques of systems development down to a fine tee, but it was the fact that they had people who knew how these techniques should be applied to our business that convinced me they were the right consultants to help us."

Two Million Accounts

The bank's operations are divided into three geographical areas, the United Kingdom, The United States of America and, of course, Ireland. Its retail division in Ireland is responsible for over two million customer accounts, about forty percent of the total market, and the Bank invests heavily in IT systems to support a sophisticated branch network extending throughout the country.

Its core systems are comprised of a series of IBM mainframes and AS/400 machines. Recently, the bank has begun developing PC systems which, based on client-server technology, are designed to give it an unrivaled customer information system. The main task facing the external change agents was to formulate a systems development approach, in partnership with the bank, which would enable them to improve their ability to take on major applications projects. "The areas we had to focus on initially were analysis, design and project management," said the external consultant who managed the project. "There were certain other areas, testing the actual delivery of solutions for instance, where the bank/s IT staff were particularly strong and where they needed limited assistance from us."

The Road Map

In common with every major clearing bank in the early 1990s, the Bank of Ireland was determined to reduce its cost income ratio. Throughout the course of the project it was clear that the bank was readying itself for a major business reengineering project to address such problems. What resulted from the work of the external consultant and the bank's IT staff was essentially an IT road map which allowed the IT staff to implement a way of working, which would allow the bank to undertake a major systems project.

Benchmarking the Human Side of IT

The leadership of the bank recognized the importance of documenting their improvement in organizational effectiveness. To accomplish their objective, they contracted with another outside consultant to administer their Job Diagnostic Survey - Information Technology. This instrument measures 28 human variables, which is about 55 percent of the typical IT budget, and compared the bank to an international database of over 200 other IT organizations. The JDS-IT helped the leadership team at the bank pinpoint some human concerns that needed to be addressed to improve the bank's culture for implementing technology driven change. To reinforce the change program, a training program was designed for all IT managers that reinforced good management practices, such as giving good feedback, and how to motivate staff to increased productivity.

Change Management Workshops

The project team set up workshops with the aim of identifying the practices that would be readily accepted and to discover the areas where resistance would be high. The workshops were conducted by the external change agent and involved about 30 IT staff who were encouraged to speak freely about their work and where they felt improvements might be made. "The workshops helped us to get into the day to day reality of how the IT staff at the bank worked," said the external consultant. "Their openness helped tremendously."

Working on the Partnership

Following on from the workshops, it took just over three months to complete the Quality Management System (QMS) with the bank's IT leadership team effectively writing the document while the external consultant exercised editorial control. "This is what we mean when we talk about partnership," says Conor O'Toole. "One of the most positive points about this project was that the bank's staff knew exactly where they needed help and they trusted the external consultant to help them in these areas. There were no major clashes over the big issues."

The QMS contained the systems development lifecycle, the standards for testing, project management and quality reviews. The next step was to bring the finished document to life with a full training program encompassing around 30 courses in total and afterwards a trial of the QMS on a live project. The bank chose a MIS project designed to help management analyze operational statistics on their Automated Teller Machine (ATM) network.

"This was a project which allowed us to assess the performance of the QMS without incurring major risk," said Conor O'Toole. "Everything went so smoothly we were then able to move on to other areas."

Confidence in Moving Forward

Following this success in managing technology driven change, the bank will now include the QMS as an integral part of its IT change strategy. Conor O'Toole concludes:

> "The integration of QMS into the daily operating processes in ISD could not have come at a more opportune time. Following our investment in the people side of our business through the Job Diagnostic Survey - Information Technology, the investment in QMS provided the hard mechanics needed to rigorously manage the software construction process. Aided by the powerful combination of QMS and the mood change generated by the JDS-IT, we have successfully delivered a completely restructured Client-Server based Branch System that provides much enhanced loan and cheque processing capability at BOI. These new systems (50 in total), were delivered to quality specifications, on time and within budgets struck 18 months earlier. We simply could not have done it 3 years ago. In reality, the work that was done with us gave us the confidence and the structures to begin to redevelop our core banking systems to deliver the transformed Bank of Ireland."

Case 2

Transforming Information Services at Technical Services

by Carol A. Norman
Major Account Manager, Telephone Express

Background of the Company

Technology Services is the centralized I/S company within a large Latin American multinational. While a number of divisions have their own I/S departments and also purchase services from external sources, about 70% of all I/S requirements within the Group are developed and delivered via Technology Services. In 1992, Technology Services consisted of approximately 400 full-time equivalents (FTE's).

About the Change Effort

In early 1992, the Group began to realize that Technology Services was not well positioned to keep delivering the services the Group would need into the next millennium. After discussing a variety of alternatives and approaches, it was agreed to form a *change team* of approximately 30 people within Technology Services, with the assistance of a consulting team. The approach was to take a *process-oriented* view of everything Technology Services did and the change team was empowered to change (whatever they felt appropriate) the processes of I/S as well as the relevant jobs, organizational structure or performance measures.

Features of the Change Effort

1) It was *wholesale & holistic* - all I/S processes were redesigned. Additionally, jobs were re-aligned to more fully support the new processes and a new (simplified) performance management system was put in place.

2) It was *vision led* - A compelling vision that everyone believed in was the driving force of the change initiative. Additionally, once the processes were designed and new tasks/roles identified to perform the processes were clear, only then did a new (and fundamentally different) organizational form emerge. Lastly, this new organizational structure was not treated as a single discrete event such as an organizational announcement, but instead a six month transition organization was utilized where people qualified for new positions based both on pervious performance and performance exhibited in new pilots. As such, pilots became a key mechanism in proving both the new way of working and qualifying people into new positions who may not otherwise had the opportunity to perform those roles due to functional specialists, historical baggage, etc.

Key Deliverables and Results

1) A new systems development process that delivered the first three projects in 40 percent less time and cost than the previous six projects before the initiative was commenced.

2) A closer relationship between I/S and the business units. Subsequent to this change initiative, one of the divisions elected to reengineer its core manufacturing process and a number of I/S consultants from Technology Services were asked to join the team based on their renewed reputation and the belief that they had newly-acquired change agent skills.

3) A customer satisfaction survey indicated a 35 percent improvement, in four months, after completing the implementation of the new customer support process.

4) A new human resource capability based on the *resource pool concept* where resource allocation was centrally done based on forward requirements from the business, availability of I/S staff, and personal career objectives. The outcome was few people had permanent employees reporting to them, instead about 80 percent of the personnel were placed in a centralized resource pool and were assigned to projects on an as-needed basis. This provided high levels of staff motivation as people's

growth need strength (GNS) was met due to job/project rotations between different technical disciplines, areas of the business, etc. This multi-skilling was also beneficial from an organizational perspective as the organization believed it would suffer from less *technical lock-in* - the phenomena where employees with key technical skill that few others know hold the organization hostage for personal gain such as pay, promotion, status, or other privileges.

Lessons Learned from this Business Process Change Effort

1) Clean up the day to day first! If you are not running a transparent I/S operations group that the business is satisfied with, delay any changes to any other area in I/S until this mopping up exercise is complete. Although not exciting and sometimes seen as low value work, this area of I/S was perceived to be the cornerstone of the business. Technology Services believed it made little sense to begin piling on new system development, I/T planning, or H/R processes and techniques until it could competently operate transparently its existing systems.

2) Peoples' ability to accept change is in direct proportion to their involvement in it. This may sound like an old adage, but the experiences at Technology Services proved that the more people were involved in the change effort, the greater their ability to join in and contribute, thus giving the initiative their personal signature through their buy-in and commitment.

3) Successful transitioning of personnel from the old organization to the new organization is enhanced if people are migrated through pilots or projects. This gives the advantage of people being able to experience the new way of working in a relatively risk-free environment before being thrown the organizational chart and told where they're sitting now and who they report to.

4) Manage the Steering Committee into leading the new organization. Too often, Steering Committees' serve as archaic ap-

proval bodies with distanced attachment from the initiatives they are to be managing. In the era of more change initiatives being led from within, the role of the Steering Committee changes from being one of approving to one of anticipating. Traditionally, Steering Committees are watching from afar and by getting them to *live the future today* we were able to prepare them for managing the new organization *before it actually arrived* instead of being caught up in the day-to-day of transition. They were waiting on the other side prepared when the organization crossed the river and met management on the other side.

5) Make explicit and communicate a set of principles to the organization which will guide the transition and implementation. These principles should outline how selection of new jobs will be done, treatment of employees and contracting personnel, how results will be monitored, if people on the change initiative will be treated differently in the transition appraisal system, and how the reward structure will change.

6) A 7 to 10 percent mobilization of I/S resources, fully dedicated to the change effort, did not diminish the organization's ability to deliver the regular work going on in parallel and customer satisfaction actually improved. In other words, we took out 35 people, full time, from a population of about 400 in the organization, and for 18 months the organization was still able to function, at the same levels of performance and customer satisfaction.

Case 3

Transforming Leadership at Household Financial Network: Taking a Pro-active Role in Enabling and Empowering the Workforce

by Roy Stansbury and Cathy Marsh
Kanbay Resources, Inc.[1]

Background of the Company

Household International Incorporated, in Prospect Heights, Illinois, provides most financial services typical consumers might need throughout their lifetime. Some of these services include home equity credit lines, secured and unsecured loans, private-label credit cards, VISA credit card accounts, and checking, saving and money market accounts. In order to provide these services in an efficient and cost-effective manner, Household International (HI) has maintained a pro-active approach to utilizing new technologies.

To achieve this objective, HI must bring all its' people in alignment with the IT goal of providing value-added services through a participatory culture. The HI vision is:

1) Our vision for Household International is to be a premier financial services provider, recognized for leadership positions in our markets and superior returns for our shareholders.

2) We will realize this vision by fully leveraging our core strengths across all of our businesses, while adhering to a value system which is strongly held throughout the company.

3) We see our core strengths as these: A culture which encourages company-wide sharing of internal competencies; centralized financial oversight which ensures effective cost management and sound investment practice; economies of scale which give us competitive advantages, agility to adjust to changing business conditions to maximize opportunities.

4) The value system which is shared throughout Household is

based on commitments to our four principal constituencies: For our employees we will provide a work environment which embraces diversity and recognizes merit, encourages personal learning and growth, fosters open communication and demonstrates respect for family needs.

About the Change Effort

The challenge facing HI is one that concerns most companies - there are no constants in the rapidly changing business environment in which they can count. In order to address this ongoing flux, HI has adopted an aggressive posture to remain on top of new technologies that allows it to respond quickly to market demands. However, this emphasis on information technology (IT) has had an impact on the organization's culture. In order to successfully implement this level of cutting-edge technology it became evident that the Household Financial Network Division (HFN) leadership take an active role guiding the process to ensure that the technological innovations address the organization's business needs. To achieve this level of alignment, the HFN leadership needed to redirect their focus from a detail oriented view to a global perspective that can accurately determine market trends.

In 1990, HFN turned to Kanbay Resources, Inc., to partner in facilitating Household's IT objectives. Kanbay's initial work centered on a Legacy Systems software reengineering project. Kanbay's contribution was so successful that the number of HFN people assigned to maintain the systems were reduced from ten to two.

Dave Barany, Household International Vice President and CIO, said:

> "I knew we were headed in the right direction, but we needed to get beyond the day-to-day management issues. The question we needed to ask was: How do we best position our organization to effectively utilize technology, while optimizing Household's business goals? To answer this we needed to move HFN management into a new stewardship mode, enabling our leadership team to focus on the long-term market-driven view,

while our staff was encouraged and empowered to concentrate on the day-to-day operations.

Since I come from a business background, my question to the technocrats always has been: Why can't we retrieve the information we need for accurate long-term planning? I knew we needed help in developing a leadership cadre that could effectively and efficiently manage our operations to provide our customer base - HI - with what it wants and needs. This depth of leadership can provide us with the strategic foresight critical to empowering our workforce to assume the tasks of developing appropriate IT systems. I know that the only constant we can count on is dynamic change. Nothing stays the same. We must equip ourselves to handle the ever-changing nature of our business and, adjust how we do business. With Kanbay's assistance, we were developing and implementing new systems, such as a client-server that would provide us a one-point of sale operation. Now, we need to look at how our people manage themselves and others in our organization."

However, Barany realized before changes could occur, HFN's technocrats needed to be attuned with HI's overall business needs, shifting from a technical-driven to a business-driven perspective. His concern centered around the need for empowering this group to interweave technological innovations with the larger demands of the marketplace. This would enable the group to think strategically, establishing the direction it should take in identifying and addressing business needs.

Barany's goal was to elevate the leadership capabilities to new plateau of understanding. This would enable the group to support its staffs as they took responsibility for recommending and solving technological problems to quickly and efficiently meet customer-based needs. He understood that there was no need for leadership to remain involved in every detail of a project. As true leaders, this same group can provide a strong infrastructure to enable others to explore creative solutions. The benefit of such a relationship lead to synergy within IT work teams.

As Kanbay took an increasingly active role in developing and implementing HFN's systems technologies, IT benefits such as decreasing processing time and redundancies of work processes, were apparent. Now, it became evident that Kanbay's organizational transformation expertise would provide the link to align the IT objectives with leadership development.

Often, people with technical expertise are excellent tacticians, but not very effective strategists. Therefore, it was necessary to help the group of 80 managers, assistant vice presidents, vice presidents and directors, begin the process of relinquishing their perceived jobs at HFN, to define and adopt the roles they must assume. For most, this is not an easy task. One that takes time to evolve and needs mentoring. Kanbay's approach was to guide the HFN leadership on its journey.

As Peter Block wrote in **Stewardship**:

> "If the structure changes but the belief system about maintaining control and consistency and predictability remains untouched, nothing fundamentally changes. When the day-to-day practices begin to change, middle managers and supervisors begin to get the feeling that they are not needed. Every discussion of partnership and self-management seems to lead to the question, What is the new role of the supervisor or manager? What do supervisors do in this empowered organization?"

Strategic Planning

These were questions Dave Barany wanted Kanbay to help his organization address. The process began in September 1993, with a one-day in-depth strategic planning session, followed by a two-day session in October (see Figure C3-1). By breaking up this first phase, participants were given additional time to reflect on the process and the journey. The objective was to cover a number of points, including:

1. examining business scenarios that HFN might face,

2. examining core competencies,

3. developing a vision,

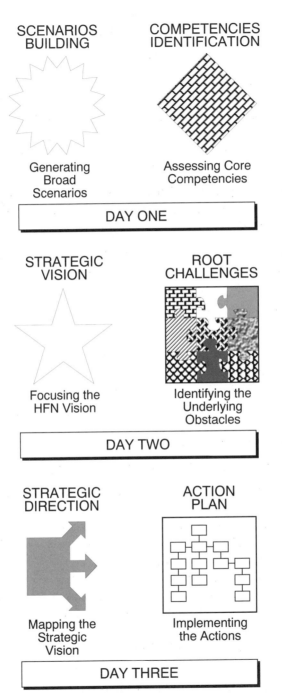

Figure C3-1. HFN Strategic Vision Process.

4. analyzing stakeholder values, and

5. taking on the initiative for the year to come.

Coming to the forefront was the recognition that leadership has to become more pro-active in exercising its core competencies (see Figure C3-2). These skills enable HFN to position itself so that operations flow smoothly. The competencies HFN must retain or develop for the future to achieve this level of operation included:

1. **Ability to partner with the business:** Our knowledge of the business and anticipation of Household International's needs leads to HFN being a value added partner.

2. **Ability to integrate systems effectively:** Our capability to select and implement the right technology solution at the right time.

3. **Ability to work as a team:** Our ability to select and keep the right people who have a sense of ownership and urgency.

To take advantage of these competencies and incorporate newly learned skills the group determined three key strategic directions to implement through 1994. They were

1. **Manage the changing technology environment,**

2. **Enable enterprise business solutions, and**

3. **Establish alternative operational patterns.**

In supporting and reinforcing this new direction, the leadership team developed a strategic vision.

As we move toward the third millennium, HFN fosters a vision as a global leader in the cost-effective creation and delivery of innovative financial products and services.

Superior management of enterprise data and architecture, profit-focused marketing strategies and a skilled, dedicated and mobile workforce will enable HFN to optimize Household's business goals.

The group also identified four challenges that might keep it from attaining this vision.

1. Undefined benefits and undeveloped marketing of enterprise business solutions,

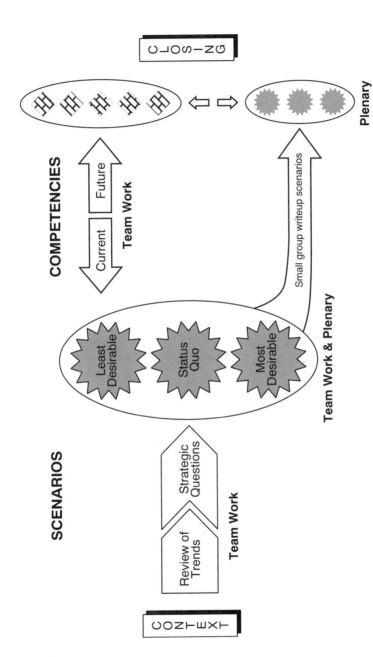

Figure C3-2. Generating Scenarios & Assessing Competencies.

2. Underdeveloped skills in managing and communicating technology life cycle,

3. Uncertain outcome of external technological trends and internal response, and

4. Inadequate response to changing workforce dynamics.

Implementation Phase

After the steps above, the leadership team agreed to move into implementation. Many at the leadership level still were having a difficulty understanding the need to let go of their traditional roles as tacticians and move on to become strategists. To move the group along on the journey, Kanbay organized a three-day session to serve as a catalyst for the leadership to step up to the changes that needed to occur, especially the cultural changes within the organization. It was critical to move the leadership into a new posture - one that empowers others to evaluate and solve technical problems that impact how products gets to the customer. To achieve this objective, Kanbay took the leadership through an intense three-stage process in June, 1994.

This phase took place during a four-day period. Critical to the success of this journey was the leadership's transformation prior to a cultural change occurring within the organization. In the first day, Kanbay had the members analyze HFN's culture within four areas:

> Rituals - what are the repetitive interactions (such as meetings) around which people organize their work?

> Status - what is valued within the organization?

> Totems - how are people recognized and rewarded?

> Taboos - what is forbidden (for what does someone lose his or her job?)

The desired culture was then discussed using the same criteria. If we had a perfect culture at Household, what would be the rituals, status, totems and taboos? This led to a discussion of what would be required to move from the current to the desired culture, and what attitudes did people need to shed or acquire. Among the functions they identified were:

needing to let go of controlling every last detail,

needing to learn to trust people more and have faith in their abilities.

By the end of that first day, participants created symbols, using various art materials, depicting what they would relinquish. They were instructed to carry this symbol around with them for the remainder of the four-day session.

The second day was devoted to questioning and confusion. The question asked was, "If I am not who I was then who am I?" This led to a deliberate look at the role of leadership, with the idea of how each leader would begin to evaluate the organization's tangibles and deal with issues of culture shift. The goal is to enable people within Household to determine what changes are necessary and then make those changes.

The third and fourth days were devoted to moving forward, looking at the next steps. In a dramatic gesture, participants burned the symbols they had been carrying for four days. This ceremony was a symbolic letting go of the past. Not only did they throw away their symbols, but participants also had to reveal what they were relinquishing. This set the stage for determining the path forward.

Since Kanbay's directive was to help HFN management build it's strategic capabilities, each session was designed to break down barriers that were restraining the group. However, many of the participants still had a hard time letting go of their past, which was effecting their ability to deliver on a strategic level. In the culture HI wants reinforced at HFN, managers must assume a facilitation posture, relative to the people with whom they work, not to projects or things as previously perceived. Managers need to internalize that their role is to empower, persuade and motivate others at Household to solve the problems. Only when they can do that will they be ready to move on to become real leaders, establishing the path for HFN's directions. And, real leadership empowers others to take the initiative and move forward.

The group was very disquieted when they realized that there

is no closure to the journey they had undertaken. Where they started with assumptions, they ended with questions. Where they started with certainties, they ended with uncertainties. And, where they started with fixed ideas, they ended with the realization that each new idea will undergo constant change.

Strategic Response

In order to keep their momentum and to build on the previous sessions, HFN agreed that additional off-site time was need to focus on specific strategic issues. This series was set for September, 1994. Primarily, it was agreed that the leadership team needed to develop strategic responses to key issues facing HFN, so that it continues to contribute to HI as an effective business partner. In essence, this was critical to reinforcing a strategic mode of thinking (see Figure C3-3).

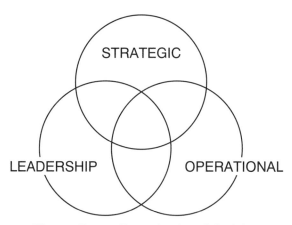

Figure C3-3. Organizational Activity.

The group spent one and one-half days, using the screen of an organization's roles - strategic, leadership and operational - as a filter to further understand the impact of strategic activity. Although some movement had been made in that direction, many entrenched ideas still had to be shed. The intent of this meeting was to demonstrate the importance for HFN to develop greater alignment with HI to achieve joint objectives. Reaching for a higher level of involvement, the group determined strategic objectives through 1997.

The meeting's outcomes were clearly articulated strategic responses and measurable milestones for key issues, agreement upon departmental ownership and commitment by all members to the successes of implementation. Several issues emphasized the need for enlarging the decision-making capabilities at HFN for 1995 through 1997. These issues include keeping pace with changes brought about by client-server technologies; establishing HI technology architecture; streamlining process, procedures that would improve response time; and ensuring the development, empowerment and recognition of HFN people as the *number one* asset.

Each of these issues already is being addressed at HFN, but they continue to need more attention. The benefits of delegating and working with staff guarantees that their alignment and attunement of people and technology decreases waste, processing time, and improves communication among all levels. These benefits bring HFN closer in alignment with HI objectives of utilizing technology to meet market demands.

The Next Step

HFN's leadership group will meet in 1995 to continue its journey to determine where they have been, where they want to go and how it continue the alignment with the HI's objectives. In tandem with this strategic alignment is the personal journey and growth all HFN leaders and individual contributors must be willing to undertake to continue this transformation.

References

1. Kanbay Resources is an information technology and organizational transformation consulting firm headquartered in Chicago, Illinois.

Index

To order additional copies of **Transforming the Mature Information Technology Organization: Reenergizing and Motivating People** (ISBN 0-9646910-0-0) please use any of the three addresses below. The cost of the book is $38.95(U.S.) plus $5 postage and packaging. For orders of 5 copies or more, the price is $32.95 each plus $3 postage and packaging. Please make all checks payable to Zawacki and Associates.

1. Internet: robertz@zawacki.com

2. Fax: 719 599 0849

3. Mailing: EagleStar Publishing
              7521 Gillen Road
              Colorado Springs, CO 80919